the now of work

BECOMING PART OF THE FUTURE-PROOF WORKFORCE

LISA MESSENGER

FOUNDER AND EDITOR-IN-CHIEF OF *COLLECTIVE HUB*

© 2020, The Messenger Group

All rights reserved. No part of this book may be reproduced in any form or by any means, electronic or mechanical, including photocopying, recording or by any information or retrieval, without prior permission in writing from the publisher. Under the Australian Copyright Act 1968 (the Act), a maximum of one chapter or 10 per cent of the book, whichever is the greater, may be photocopied by any educational institution for its educational purposes provided that the education institution (or the body that administers it) has given a remuneration notice to Copyright Agency Limited (CAL) under the Act.

Any views and opinions expressed herein are strictly the author's own and do not represent those of The Messenger Group.

A catalogue record of this book is available from the National Library of Australia.

Messenger, Lisa. The Now Of Work
ISBN 978-0-6485872-4-8
First published in 2020 by The Messenger Group Pty Ltd
Project Management: @em.lystudio
Editing: Cindy Donato & Grace Potter
Sub Editing: Emily Ditchburn
Creative Direction and Design: @em.ly studio
Photography of Lisa: Jade Jeffries
Distribution Enquiries: lisam@collectivehub.com

This is proudly a Lisa Messenger product, lisamessenger.com
Collective Hub, collectivehub.com

DISCLAIMER
The content of this book is to serve as a general overview of matters of interest and is not intended to be comprehensive, nor does it constitute advice in any way. This book is a compilation of one person's ideas, concepts, ideologies, philosophies and opinions. You should carry out your own research and/or seek your own professional advice before acting or relying on any of the information displayed in this book. The author, The Messenger Group Pty Ltd and its related entities will not be liable for any loss or damage (financial or otherwise) that may arise out of your improper use of, or reliance on, the content of this book. You accept sole responsibility for the outcomes if you choose to adopt and/or use the ideas, concepts, ideologies, philosophies and opinions within the content of this book.

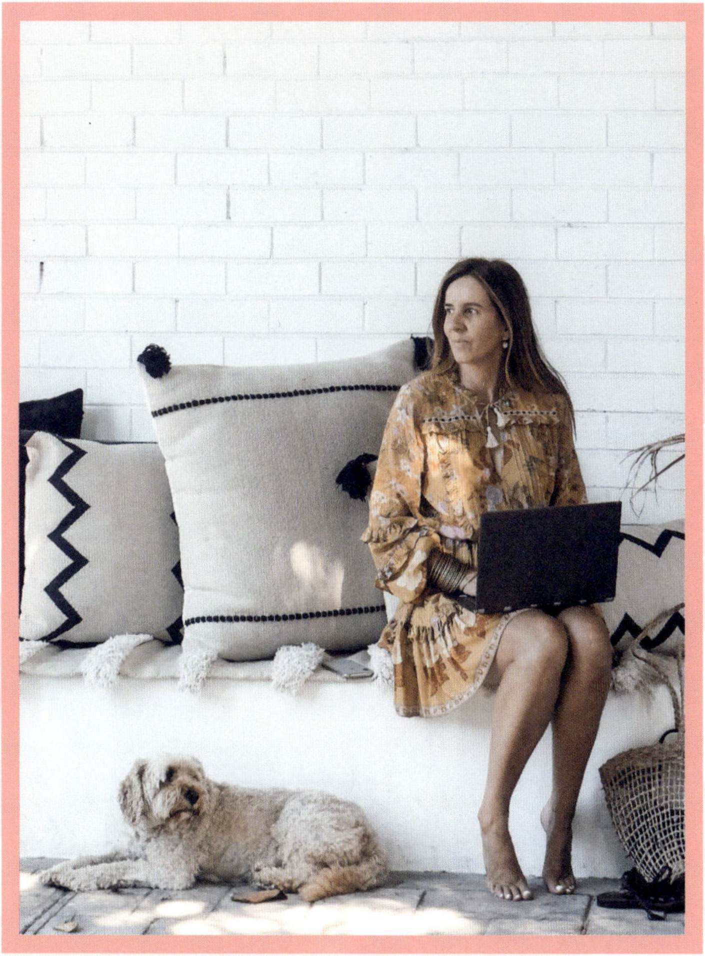

> There are no mistakes in life, only lessons. There is no such thing as a negative experience, only opportunities to grow, learn and advance along the road of self-mastery. From struggle comes strength. Even pain can be a wonderful teacher.

– ROBIN SHARMA

CONTENTS

INTRODUCTION	8
CHAPTER 1: HAPPENING NOW	26
CHAPTER 2: YOUR WHY	78
CHAPTER 3: BLAZING A TRAIL	100
CHAPTER 4: FLIP FEAR	122
CHAPTER 5: THE LOGISTICS	146
CHAPTER 6: LOCATION FREEDOM	184
CHAPTER 7: YOUR WORKFORCE	226
CHAPTER 8: YOUR TOOLKIT	264
CHAPTER 9: DISCIPLINE, RITUALS ROUTINES AND BOUNDARIES	304
EXTRAS+	362

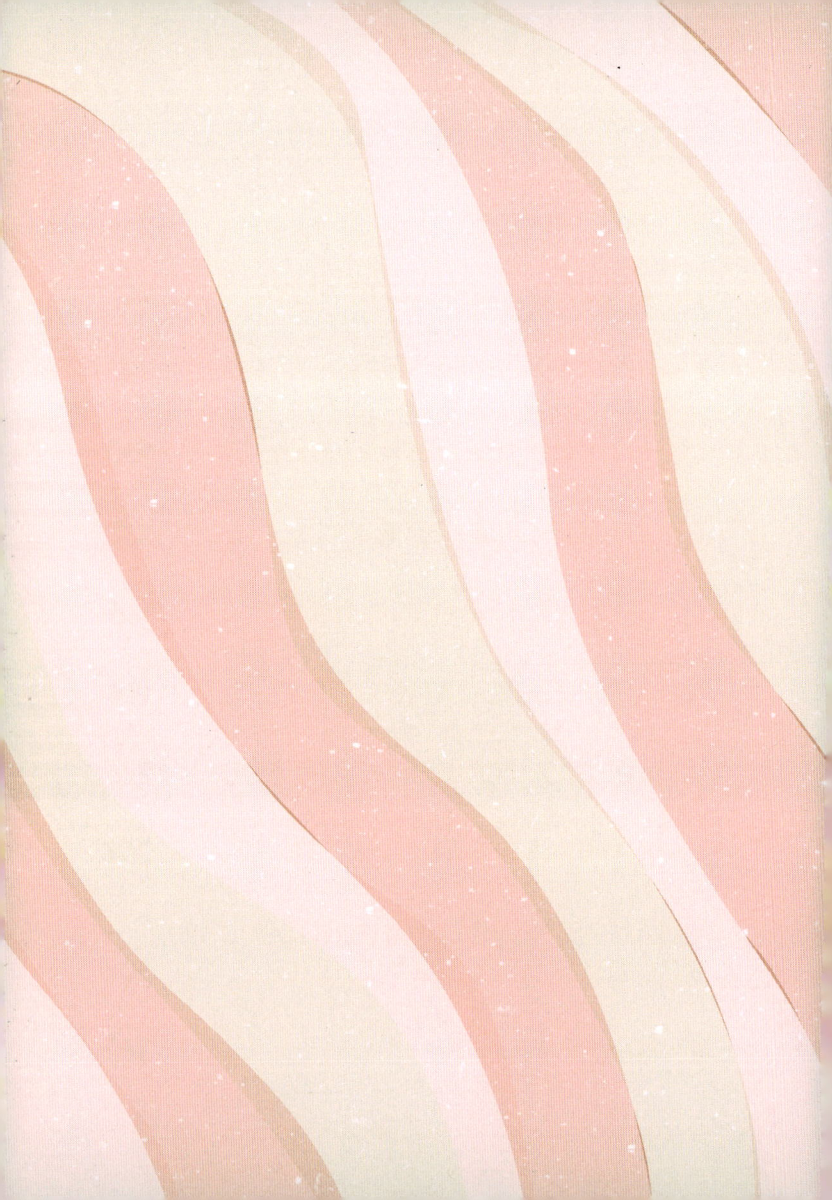

Let the now of work begin...

INTRODUCTION

THE WORLD AS WE KNOW IT HAS CHANGED.

Not even halfway through 2020, we found ourselves amidst the global pandemic of COVID-19. In just a short amount of time we have seen a huge collective shift to **new ways of living.** This pandemic has upended us and uprooted us, and challenged us as a world like we have never been challenged before in our lifetimes.

As humans, it is our instinct not only to survive, but to thrive, so that we can handle whatever life throws our way. While we can't control what happens in the outside world, we can control how we respond to it.

Throughout my life, I have ducked and weaved my way through plenty of challenging situations. These experiences have taught me that being divergent is good. Moving away from what was expected of me, following my intuition and **being daring and disruptive not only opened up my world, but opened the world up to me.**

It can be so easy for us to get caught up in the challenge and be overcome with all the doubts and fears that come along with it.

I know – I have done this my fair share of times. However, when we do control our response to challenges, keep an open mind and think about how we can do things outside of the box, we open ourselves up to so many possibilities and new ways of doing things which we might not have even considered before.

I have been called the face and voice of the nomadic workforce for the past few years. *Now, I'm not exactly sure about that!* But what I do know is this – the future of work that we have all been talking about for the past few years is **happening now.**

We have been spending so long gazing into this horizon of work where we have location freedom, time freedom and can control our schedules, and COVID-19 was the push to make us stop dreaming about it happening in the future 'some time' and execute it NOW.

Normally, shifting from the office to working from home is a longer, smoother transition with more planning ahead of time. Due to COVID-19, everyone had to instantly navigate their way through this complex journey to working from home practically overnight.

With all the differing information, opinions and misinformation out there about working remotely, I have created this book to help you not only make sense of it all, but adapt, thrive and emerge successfully.

I have been doing this working from home thing for about 730 days longer than everyone else who was flung into it unannounced. Running multiple global businesses across various verticals with hundreds of team members means that I have learned a lot about working remotely. I'm sometimes even referred to as a 'professional pivoter' of life – the transition of working from anywhere for myself and my team was perhaps one of the hugest pivots I've ever made.

While all the article lists with tips for helping you work from home can be helpful, I have first-hand experience of shifting an entire business and teams to working from wherever. I want to use my expertise and experience to help you navigate this huge change.

Throughout this book, you'll learn strategies to get your mindset, your skill set, your technology, logistics and all the disciplines, rituals, routines and boundaries in place so you'll not just survive in this new remote workforce, but feel **strong, equipped and supported** during the recovery of this global pandemic.

HOW DID I GET TO WHERE I AM TODAY?

After 11 years of having my own businesses, I launched *Collective Hub* in 2013 as a print magazine. It quickly became a global sensation and was available in 37 countries.

Today, it has evolved into a true multimedia brand that encompasses engaging digital content, bespoke events, strategic collaborations and unique product extensions. The mission of *Collective Hub* has always been the same, no matter the medium – uplift and empower people to live their lives to the fullest and to ignite human potential.

My business got 'sick' in 2017. It may have even completely crumbled beneath me had I not made the toughest decision of my life – to discontinue the print magazine and essentially break the business until just the bones were left. I had to think differently and drastically change everything in order to remake it in a more sustainable way. We decentralised the entire business in real-time, let go of the huge overhead cost of an office and moved the remaining team to **working online from anywhere in the world.**

After 17 years of working in my brick-and-mortar office, it was **not easy,** but that tough decision **saved me, my business and my amazing staff**, who are more productive and passionate than ever about the work we do. It turbocharged the need to work from home. No longer was it a luxury for some, but it became a necessity for all.

I used to freak out at the thought of people working outside of the office. For years, my absolute, inbuilt belief was that if my team weren't at their desks in the same building as I was, they simply weren't being productive. Now, I've shown myself that **this couldn't be further from the truth.**

Suffice to say, decentralising was one of the best decisions I've ever made. Working when we felt like it and wherever we wanted meant that we had freedom. We only meet when it's important. We stay in our lane and know what we need to get done. We're not in the office looking over one another's shoulders, getting involved in things that we really have no business in, and we're all on the same page. I couldn't be happier, and neither could my team.

This age of the digital nomad offered a beautiful blend of both work and life – no balancing act required. It made me wonder why we hadn't tried this before, and certainly why everyone wasn't also doing the same. It was like we'd hit a goldmine that not many other people knew about yet.

Fast forward to now and the world is suddenly, extremely sick, driving instant change in the way we live and work.

I love the freedom of working from wherever. If you roll it out right, you can successfully transition either personally as a solopreneur, or as part of your workforce.

Whatever your situation, you can create the working life of your dreams.

"

Look at the beautiful skies and everybody is talking about Mother Nature being regenerated.

> So, latch onto the positive and live in the moment.

– POONAM SAPRA

Let's start with the nitty-gritty.

WHAT ARE THE ROADBLOCKS?
WHAT ARE THE PROS AND CONS?
ARE THERE PSYCHOLOGICAL AND EMOTIONAL CONSIDERATIONS THAT NEED ADDRESSING?
WHAT DO YOU NEED TO DO TO MAKE THIS WORK FOR YOU, YOUR TEAM AND YOUR BUSINESS?

From mindset to financials to technology and logistics, I've been there, doing that, and am excited to share my learnings and tricks of the trade with you all in this book.

I have already forged this path back in 2017. Before COVID-19, my book, *Work From Wherever*, rolled out the blueprint for entrepreneurs and employees to create a new lifestyle of location freedom and become digital nomads.

During the pandemic, my team and I pivoted to meet the new challenges and realities of working in quarantine, and so did hundreds of thousands of teams around the world.

We realised that everything we had learned over the past few years was exactly what everyone needs to know right now for our new reality.

This book will become your work from home manual – a practical, actionable how-to guide for creating your own location freedom, whether that be as a solopreneur, entrepreneur, intrapreneur or leading your entire workforce into this new state of play.

WHY DO I USE THE WORD PLAY?

Because that's what it should be. **Play your best game. Play as hard as you can. Throw everything into it.** Make it hard play, not hard labour, because that's the magic of working remotely, especially in tough economic times. Keep it light, and you'll make light work of moving operations to the remote space.

My learnings are now yours, so you can successfully transition your team to work from anywhere without missing a beat. I'll equip you with a well-stocked toolkit of rituals, routines, structures, disciplines and resources to help you get the most out of the shift. Whether you're a freelancer, working in a corporation or anything in-between, the principles for success are the same.

When I made the conscious decision in 2017 to lead my team to work from wherever, I was used to an office giving me a sense of purpose every day and having coworkers I loved and adored to hug and high-five in the morning right there with me. I enjoyed having buddies to ideate with, reimagine with, bounce ideas around with and come up with projects for the future with.

listen here

**The time is right now.
Play your best game.
Throw everything into it.
Play hard.
Make it hard play
– not hard labour.**

**Keep it light and you'll
make light work.**

@LISAMESSENGER

> **Your greatest self has been waiting your whole life; don't make it wait any longer.**

– STEVE MARABOLI

I loved having a great culture and shared sense of purpose.
I know that many of you would have been the same. The office model is all we've known for decades, and we've also been taught that it's the only model that works.

When the shift happened and the team decentralised, I suddenly felt isolated. There was a part of me that felt like I had failed. I used to have so many doers and implementers around me taking care of a lot of my technology and administration needs, and **suddenly it was just me and my laptop, staring blankly into the abyss.** If I had a problem with setting up an online tool on my laptop, I would have to be the one to fix it. I was also back to being responsible for business administration tasks and setting up our online systems for working together as a team. I was jittery about how I would adapt and how I would learn all these new things.

HOW WOULD I CONNECT?
HOW WOULD I TRACK PRODUCTIVITY?
HOW WOULD I STAY ON TOP OF MY TO-DO LISTS?

As the leader of my team, I had to have it down-pat so I could then roll it out to everyone else.

As COVID-19 loomed and started spreading across seas from country to country, businesses began to take action to protect their teams and moved everyone to working from home.

I heard the jitters of the world, all joining the chorus of "how?" that used to be my mantra back then. I had spent a couple of years setting up all my rituals and routines, and we were all humming along perfectly. I felt happier, more connected, tech-savvy and productive than ever.

Then, almost overnight, Australia was in lockdown and I found myself in quarantine with my partner. After years of getting into our own groove as a couple and getting used to our usual routine, this briefly brought with it a whole other set of unforeseen issues around cohabiting. As much as we love our partners, living in each other's pockets 24/7 and dealing with the noise, disruptions and battles for office real estate can be extremely challenging.

Most of us are also not used to spending this much time with the same person, having previously gone into an office five days a week. **It's a cake with many layers of chaos.**

We've all seen the meme about Cheryl circulating on social media – it was 'Cheryl' who left the dirty cups around, and it was 'Cheryl' who was screaming down the phone when I was trying to quietly write. It seems 'Cheryl' has been responsible for many disputes in our new home workplaces as we all grapple with how to find the sweet spot of sharing our space with her every day.

Through the frustrations, hassles and learning curves of the new way of working, **I'm here to tell you that it is all okay.** I've been there. The things that I was once fearful of (and, in some cases, sent me into a complete petrified meltdown) are now 100 percent okay. I worked through the problems, learned what I needed to and found solutions.

We learn, we adapt and we grow.

Let's pivot and hit that curveball right out of the park. The virus was an uninvited game-changer, but we're here and we're tough, so I say – game on.

COVID-19 may have even made this our forever work model – who knows! Gearing up for working from home is smart, no matter where we all land on the other side of this.

This book is loosely based on its predecessor *Work from Wherever* and shares a little of the same content but it's much more practical, up-to-date with a lot more actionable strategies to help you NOW.

In this book you'll find worksheets, or as I prefer to call them, 'playsheets', sprinkled throughout, to ensure you're taking notes, making progress, moving forward and creating an actionable strategy that is **right and relevant for you.**

I know, I know, I'm giving you homework already, but I really want you to get as much value as possible out of this book and walk away with a plan that you can put into immediate action. First up, to get you thinking differently, use the first playsheet to list all possible roadblocks that could possibly get in the way of decentralising your office. This is the time to get real about yourself and your situation.

ARE YOU LACKING IN TECHNOLOGY KNOW-HOW?
ARE YOU AFRAID YOU WON'T MAKE NEW BUSINESS CONNECTIONS WITHOUT BEING ABLE TO MEET PEOPLE IN-PERSON?
WHAT ABOUT LOGISTICS AND SUPPLY CHAINS?
WHAT DO YOU DO ABOUT OFFICE CULTURE?
HOW WOULD YOU MANAGE STAFF FEARS, OR YOUR OWN FEARS?

Ask yourself what has the potential to go wrong. When you know what the challenges are before they come up, you can plan ahead and have a solution ready to go.

Now, you're ready to really kick into creating the life you've always dreamed of. It's time to get you into the now (and possibly forever) of work.

x Lisa

@LisaMessenger

we learn.
we adapt.
we grow.

take note

Happy workers are more productive. When they have the freedom to choose their lifestyle and optimise their routines, they are far more content and therefore perform better at work.

chapter one

HAPPENING NOW

EMBRACE THE TREND AND STAY IN THE GAME.

9-11 CHANGED THE WORLD.
NOW, COVID-19 HAS SENT THE WORLD HOME.

Almost overnight, working from home went from a trend to a mandate for business. Before, the people who worked from home were the unusual ones. **Now, working from home has become our new norm.** Together, we are sharing the positives and the challenges, and we're seeing everyone jumping to recount their experience and whether they're loving it or finding it one of the hardest things they've ever had to do.

What are the positives? For you, it might be that working to your own schedule creates more space for your routine, like exercising and meditating and taking care of the kids. Perhaps you hate mornings and are most productive in the late afternoon and early evening. Manage your time so you can start late and work late. If peak-hour traffic isn't your jam, then gaining an hour a day is a gift. For the workforce that's bogged down with end-to-end meetings and little time to deliver the actual work, then working from home without distractions could take your team to the next level of productivity as they have more time on their hands to focus on execution.

What are your gifts that you're bringing to this new table (or desk)?

LET'S DRILL DOWN HOW YOU WORK BEST.

For many, the move to working from wherever is a lifestyle or career choice. For others, it's been forced on you and will require some big adjustments in the way you work.

Wherever you've come from and whatever the situation, this transition will show you how you actually work best and provide so many opportunities for growth to come out of the challenge.

> **Not all storms come to disrupt your life.**
>
> **Some come to clear your path.**

– ANON

the work archetypes

Here are six archetypes that can help guide your transition. If you've read *Work From Wherever*, this is one of the few sections that is similar, but this time we've added a lot more substance. Get to know who you are, your strengths and how you thrive, and you can design the ultimate work from home context to deliver your best work – for your company, or for yourself.

THE ENTREPRENEUR

These guys might have run a business, they may be transitioning from full-time to 'whenever time', and they have big ideas that are their ticket to freedom. They may not feature in *Forbes* (yet), but they work to live the life they want – untethered and without limits, whenever and wherever they want.

HOW DOES THE ENTREPRENEUR WORK?

With inspiration as their key motivator, they can work nights, weekends, on holidays...sometimes they even work in their sleep dreaming up their next idea! An entrepreneur's creativity and laptop never switch off.

They're usually early adopters of trending communication apps so they can better connect with their teams in super casual but super effective ways. Flexible, nimble and professional pivoters, entrepreneurs thrive in chaos and see opportunities and solutions where others only see problems.

Technically and creatively, the entrepreneur is all over it.

Are you a risk-taker with big ideas who takes bold action, embraces the latest technological innovations, turns problems into opportunities and can work independently or as the CEO?

Entrepreneurs, you are probably stepping into your own during this time and beyond, finding ways to pivot and create faster than most. We applaud you.

archetype two
THE EMERGING ENTREPRENEUR

These are the entrepreneurial thinkers who are a short way into their journey. They've taken the leap and have bucketloads of energy and passion to fuel their vision.

They are completely inspiring.

Emerging entrepreneurs are often under-resourced, but are, themselves, extremely resourceful. Keeping overheads down by saving on office space frees up valuable dollars for the projects they're passionate about and, as they're not chained to a desk, they work freely.

HOW DOES THE EMERGING ENTREPRENEUR WORK?

You'll often find the emerging entrepreneur hot-desking in a coworking space or their favourite cafe. Networking breakfasts are food for thought (literally!). These guys know the answer to any question is a croissant away, and they're hungry.

You'll often find them sharing their tips on forums or Twitter, as they love the freedom of being able to work from wherever and want to share it with as many people as possible so that they can also see the light.

Are you bravely on your way to success?
Do you see your naivety as a blessing because often it's what you don't know that gets you ahead?
Are you always visualising a better future?

Introvert or extrovert, you have an appetite for networking because you know socialising with like-minded start-uppers bears fruit.

I love emerging entrepreneurs – you guys are already thinking about what's next. Post-pandemic recovery will be grand with the new world in your hands.

archetype three
THE BLOGGER/INFLUENCER

Social royalty, these creative spirits post their way to the top of the social media ladder... and then post their resignation letter to the boss.

They've built up enough equity in their own brand to be their own boss, and they know the value of the service they are creating. The world is their postable oyster.

> *Social marketing* ELIMINATES *the middlemen, providing brands the* UNIQUE *opportunity to have a* DIRECT *relationship with their* CUSTOMERS.
>
> – BRYAN WEINER

HOW DOES THE BLOGGER/INFLUENCER WORK?

The blogger/influencer's habitat is a hive of happenings, often handsomely sponsored by hashtag *insert brand*.

These social creatures buzz where there's buzz around them – the gym, bustling cafes or fundraisers. They are the masters of the social media universe and their superpower is engagement.

Virtual assistants, influencer talent agencies and tomorrow's apps all work for Team Influencer, and they're trending.

Are you the voice of your global tribe?
Hell, not just the voice, but the face, mind, body and soul of a culture you love sharing your knowledge with?

You are our communicators, keeping everyone sharing and caring and moving the conversation along. Keep doing your thing!

archetype four
THE BOSS/MANAGER

These guys are upper management hovering between two working worlds.

They want to be liberated, but have one toe in the corporate workplace and one in the ocean.

The boss/manager explores the balance between physically being there and working remotely.

They are employees in the corporate world or a start-up, but can see the benefits of a totally decentralised workplace.

HOW DOES THE BOSS/MANAGER WORK?

A full calendar of meetings, problems with the servers and constant disruptions often hinder their productivity – there are pain points.

However, the boss/manager thrives with people and has the skills to lead their teams through anything, whether that be a standard work day or a global pandemic.

Are you generous with your free time and like helping others achieve their potential?
Are you very content working for a company that aligns with your values and desires and are ready for the next steps of moving operations to a decentralised workforce?

You are our now, and you're nailing it!

archetype five
THE NEW GEN

New gen can change the world.

They're young, they care, and they only work if it aligns with their purpose. Technology is their wand and they learn tricks that they can do on their iPhones that will conjure a magical career.

There's no smoke and mirrors with new gen.

These forward-thinkers launch start-ups on their gap year and innovate companies while they're interning.

The first trick they ever learned was how to bend time to fit their lifestyle. They know time is as fluid as the sea, and there's oceans of it.

HOW DOES THE NEW GEN WORK?

A new gen isn't afraid to roll up their sleeves and hit the court. They think quickly on their feet and are complete opportunists. They know the latest i-gadget is worth queuing for, because those in the queue are ahead of the game.

They bankroll their box of tricks through creative salary negotiations – or even better, they invent an app that will pay for it, then invest the profits in their next venture.

Are you a master slashie (e.g. entrepreneur/ blogger/app developer)?
Do you have limited funds, or do you have a magical money generator?

Wiley, crafty inventors like you bring so much value to everyone's lives, so keep creating! We are lapping it up.

archetype six
THE INTRAPRENEUR

These guys are the solution.

The intrapreneur is that staff member who thinks differently, challenges the status quo and asks questions that forge, or adapt to, change.

The global pandemic forced the business world into cardiac arrest. In a heartbeat, it all changed. These divergent, innovative thinkers are an organisation's critical care unit who CPR the business back to life.

The intrapreneur is vital as we turbocharge into the future – they are the future. They are one-of-a-kind champions of change who boldly captain their own careers, or lead their company into new frontiers with their fantastic ideas, always imagining the possibilities, creating and innovating.

The intrapreneur is an absolute star in an ever-changing universe.

HOW DOES THE INTRAPRENEUR WORK?

The intrapreneur works in an office, nine to five, Monday to Friday. However, they never really clock off.

Free time is an opportunity to upskill with TED Talks, webinars and masterclasses that nourish their need to grow. They use autonomous technology to help them develop a side hustle, and they bring valuable discoveries to the workplace so that they, and their team, can kick butt.

In your first month on the job, did you enthusiastically email your ideas to your boss?
Do you see problems as puzzles to solve?
Do you respect the hierarchy of roles, but with a measured dose of courageous rebellion so you can change it up?

Intrapreneurs have a pinch of professional punk in them, and they punch well above their weight. It's the intrapreneur who will get our world back on its axis. You are heroes!

TAKE THE CHALLANGE. YOU CAN DO IT.

@LISAMESSENGER

Those are just six archetypes – there are more. Let's also not forget the solopreneur, which can be any of these operators, only with a focus on flying solo. Remember, one-size-fits-all doesn't fit most.

Knowing where you are and how you work is really helpful in designing your 'new-look' work day. Use these archetypes as a guide to see where you might fit, but don't pigeonhole yourself. For instance:

DO YOU ALREADY HAVE A PASSIVE INCOME AND SOLID NETWORK?

ARE YOU AN EMERGING ENTREPRENEUR WITH FEW OVERHEADS?

ARE YOU LEADING YOUR WORKFORCE INTO WORKING REMOTELY FOR NOW, OR COULD IT BE A FOREVER MOVE?

Identify which archetype you generally fit into. Then, get out a pen and your notebook, turn to a new page and just sit for a moment with your eyes closed. Put your office routine out of your mind. Put your current routine out of your mind.

THINK FOR A MOMENT – WHAT DOES YOUR IDEAL WORKDAY LOOK LIKE?
WHAT TIME WOULD YOU START SO THAT YOU CAN WORK BEST?
WHERE ARE YOU WORKING – THE HOME OFFICE, OUTSIDE, AT A STANDING DESK?
WHEN WOULD YOU TAKE BREAKS AND WHAT WOULD YOU DO WITH THOSE BREAKS TO KEEP PRODUCTIVE?

Write it down, and get to know the way that you work, not the way that you've been taught to work.

take note

It might seem silly at first, but creating your routine and sticking to it will provide clarity, drive, motivation and passion. Every day you implement your routine and check off your to-do lists, you're a little closer to reaching your goals. I know, some days are tough, but these are the days where your routine is the MOST important. Even if you feel like slumping around in bed all day, take the leap and get out, make a healthy brekky and slowly get through your routine as best as you can. By the end of the day, you can give yourself a massive pat on the back for getting through it!

> **Wherever you are, be there totally.**
>
> **If you find your here and now intolerable and it makes you unhappy, you have three options: remove yourself from the situation, change it, or accept it totally.**

If you want to take responsibility for your life, you must choose one of those three options, and you must choose now.

Then accept the consequences.

𝟗𝟗

– ECKHART TOLLE

1
PLAY

play hard

WE CAN LEARN SOMETHING FROM EVERY TYPE OF PERSON AND PERSONALITY.

Research and list one of each of the six archetypes, along with three reasons why you admire them and what qualities you could emulate. These can be people in your immediate network, mentors, or people you respect in business. Anyone!

#1 - THE ENTREPRENEUR:

Name: _____

Why I admire this person:
1. _____
2. _____
3. _____

Their best qualities that I can emulate:

_____
_____

2 - THE EMERGING ENTREPRENEUR:

Name: _____

Why I admire this person:
1. _____
2. _____
3. _____

Their best qualities that I can emulate:
_____
_____

#3 - THE BLOGGER/INFLUENCER:

Name: _____

Why I admire this person:
1. _____
2. _____
3. _____

Their best qualities that I can emulate:
_____
_____

4 - THE BOSS/MANAGER:

Name: _____

Why I admire this person:
1. _____
2. _____
3. _____

Their best qualities that I can emulate:
_____
_____

#5 - THE NEW GEN:

Name: _____

Why I admire this person:
1. _____
2. _____
3. _____

Their best qualities that I can emulate:
_____
_____

6 - THE INTRAPRENEUR:

Name: _____

Why I admire this person:
1. _____
2. _____
3. _____

Their best qualities that I can emulate:

_____
_____

> *Never regret being a GOOD person, to the wrong people. Your behavior says EVERYTHING about you, and their behavior says ENOUGH about them.*
>
> – MARC & ANGEL

How did that feel?
___
___

How is your mindset feeling now?
___
___

Are you excited about possibilities and the future?
___
___

Notes:
___
___
___
___
___
___
___
___
___

you are 100%

brilliant &
amazing

CASE STUDY

Facebook HQ

The COVID-19 emergency forced the epic-scale, work from home roll-out of one of the hugest teams we know of – the Facebook HQ workforce.

What were the communication challenges, considerations, logistics and solutions?

I reached out to Jacquie Ford, Operations Lead of Creative X at Facebook, who gave me insight into how the Facebook team has managed this transition.

What did they do?

They outsourced – not staff, not people, not projects, but technology.

To keep both large and small teams efficient, informed and connected, they used online applications such as **Workplace** and **WorkChat.**

Think enterprise versions of Facebook and Messenger, but for your workmates.

These are brilliant tools!

Workplace leverages all of the key features of Facebook, such as your feed, status updates and the ability to create groups, plus it lets you create things like to-do lists, documents and share files.

The real magic of **Workplace** is the ability to build community within your organisation.

We are in a revolution. Just as the industrial revolution changed everything, we are also tooling up, but this time our tools are technology.

For us at *Collective Hub*, **Zoom**, **Asana**, **Slack**, **Google Documents**, **Microsoft Teams** and **Dropbox** are the tools we all use to work every single day.

The Facebook workforce were able to stay connected through using their own tools.

TOOL UP AND STAY CONNECTED

Utilising these technologies and finding the ones that work for you and your team is so important to avoid stress and help everyone maximise their work time.

At Facebook, they set up work chats specifically for working out at home, which allowed the team to share motivational tips, create their own at-home workouts and inspire each other to keep moving and exercising during the day.

Not only was that great for keeping them connected and social, it was also instilling a positive habit that is especially important for anyone working from home.

Think about it – a social workforce like Facebook suddenly dispersed. It was vital to maintain and continue to build their community, otherwise some members of the team could have found themselves feeling really isolated and disconnected.

Facebook literally is community – that's their bread and butter. **They were all over this.**

Collective Hub is also a community, even though my team is literally anywhere in the world working from wherever. We've got freelancers from Manhattan to Wagga Wagga, but we are a hub, a team, and, most importantly, **we're connected no matter where we are in the world.**

WHAT ARE SOME OF THE COMPLEXITIES YOUR ORGANISATION COULD FACE?

Let's start with the human factor. Respecting our differences, our personal home environments and situations requires that you adjust expectations. Response times may need to be more fluid. You'll need to bring empathy into the workplace of yourself and your team. After all, you are now an invited guest in their home, so traditional workday hours may not be reasonable.

As an example, those with children will likely be their productive best after the kids have gone to bed. Remember that BBC live broadcast of Professor Robert Kelly looking so tailored and professional to the nation, when suddenly a playfully precocious child burst into the shot? That was pretty funny, and the perfect reminder that we are human and our homes are where we get to be our authentic selves.

I can't tell you how many dogs, cats and kids have made impromptu appearances on seemingly rigid Zoom calls, and **I couldn't love it more.** It introduces the human, vulnerable element and, just like that, we're all relatable. It's good for business.

take note

Be professional, but don't be perfect. Too often we put this unachievable expectation on ourselves to be perfect all the time at work with everything we say and do. We often don't want to make a fool of ourselves in front of the boss or a potential new partner during a Zoom meeting, which is fair enough. However, we're all humans (including your boss!) and during a global pandemic, no one is expecting you to be perfect at all. We all know that life happens and we're all in similar situations as we work our way through finding our new normal.

Now, it's time to talk about another beast – meetings.

It's a topic that will always spark debates in the workplace. Some people swear that nearly all meetings are unproductive, while a huge portion of other people's roles is to be in meetings and strategise with team members.

Some workplaces spend many a brainstorming session trying to crack the elusive code of making meetings as efficient and productive as possible. The problem with meetings is that we can get into a mindset of thinking every single one is essential, and then suddenly it's 4pm and you haven't got a single thing done all day.

I remember the endless meetings that chewed up our days. Not anymore! It's time to get familiar with shared documents and multi-edit surfaces like **Workplace**, **Google Drive**, **Trello**, **Quip** and **SharePoint** for collaborations. All of these tools will get your team work from home fit and collaborating on projects digitally in no time, meaning that you won't have to spend as much time in meetings talking about projects and can instead focus on just getting them done. Hallelujah!

Remember, we're not giving up anything. Instead, we're reinventing, innovating, pivoting, zigging, zagging and navigating new terrain. If anything, tooling up will make your working life better while giving back time to the time-poor.

STREAMLINE YOUR MEETINGS

Ask yourself – do I really need to be in this meeting? Unless it's absolutely necessary, try to minimise your involvement in meetings! If the problem can be resolved with a quick email, do that instead.

Establish somebody to chair the meeting. This person will be in charge of minutes and agenda. Having someone sticking to the program will keep everyone more efficient!

Begin the meeting with an outcome. What do you need to have achieved or decided by the end of the meeting?

Focus, focus, focus. Before your meeting, take three deep breaths to centre your mind and focus. Being present will help your meeting move faster!

Aim to finish five minutes early. That way, you're not rushing to your next commitment and are honouring everyone's valuable time.

PROJECT SELF-CARE

It's a fact that some will find transitioning a lot harder than others. **We're all different,** and that's a good thing.

Think about ways you can help the team to establish good mental health projects. For me, I need nature. With so much coming at me all the time, I'm only human and can get overwhelmed. Hitting pause to take a walk, sit under a tree or run off that pizza that somehow made its way into my mouth are my non-negotiables.

Working from wherever means doing whatever to take care of number one. Give yourself and your team permission to indulge in something nourishing.

Love yourself FIRST,
and EVERYTHING *else falls into line.*
You REALLY *have to love yourself*
to get ANYTHING *done in this world.*

– LUCILLE BALL

PRACTISE SELF-CARE

Take a walk – A simple 20-minute walk outside in the sunshine can do wonders for your day. Allowing your body fresh air and exercise will create lots of positive change.

Meditate – It takes a little practice, but practice makes perfect! Try starting with just five or 10 minutes a day, if you need some help there's plenty of free apps you can download to guide you.

Do your favourite exercise – It's so important to find exercise that you actually enjoy doing, you'll feel happier and achieve better results!

Dedicate 'me-time' – Whether you're a fan of podcasts, love reading, or enjoy a bubble bath with some wine and candles, make the time to do it!

Have a dance break – If you're feeling in a bit of a funk or just a bit bored and tired, turn on your favourite tune and dance to it in your living room.

The workforce of now works from home.

WHAT DOES THAT FEEL LIKE?

There are so many positives I can't even count, but there are also pain points.

If we feel like we're always 'on', then we're not taking care of our mental and physical wellbeing. We're always in fight or flight mode, without spending time in rest and digest mode.

With so many communications and to-dos hitting us from an array of different platforms, we have to draw a mental health line in the sand. Particularly now that we're bringing work into our home, it's more crucial than ever to establish boundaries, otherwise we become overworked and burnt-out.

Find what feels good for you and make sure you're dedicating time to properly looking after yourself.

Fill your own cup up so you can continue to live your life to your fullest potential.

> "Don't sacrifice yourself too much, because if you sacrifice too much there's nothing else you can give, and nobody will care for you."

— KARL LAGERFELD

1.1

PLAY

YOU CAN'T LOVE ANYONE OR ANYTHING UNLESS YOU LOVE YOU FIRST.

As I touched on earlier in this chapter, self-care is so important to maintain healthy relationships in life, work, friendships and partners. Taking time to let you be you, enjoy the things you love and give your body, mind and soul what it needs to shine, should never be taken advantage of. So, let's delve a little deeper into the **now** of self-care in our current working arrangements.

List some tangible and actionable ways you can help yourself, or your team practise healthy mental distancing from work/home/life balance.

_____
_____
_____
_____
_____
_____

Make a list of all the things that make you feel the happiest version of you:

1. _____
2. _____
3. _____
4. _____
5. _____
6. _____
7. _____
8. _____

Who are the people you can rely on to give you positive energy and motivation? List your support people here:

1. _____
2. _____
3. _____
4. _____
5. _____
6. _____
7. _____
8. _____

A WEEK OF SELF-CARE

Plan your next week out to include a self-care activity each day. Hold yourself accountable to make it happen. Consider how you feel going into the week and then make a note how you feel once you've completed the full seven days. **Do you feel better? More energised? More in love with yourself?**

MON

TUE

WED

THU

FRI

SAT

SUN

Notes/comments/takeaways/ideas:

LOVE YO'SELF

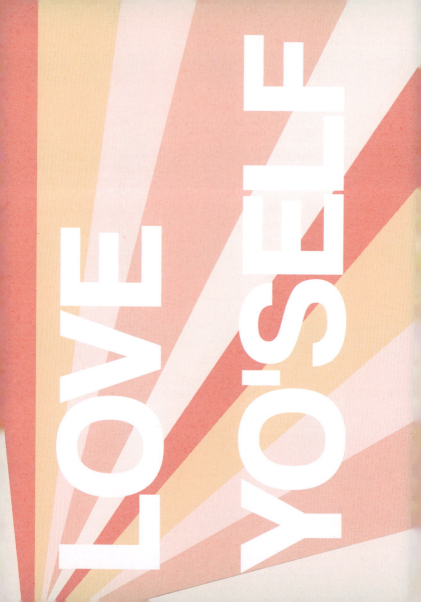

> **I no longer force things. What flows, flows. What crashes, crashes. I only have space and energy for the things that are meant for me.**

@LISAMESSENGER

chapter two

YOUR WHY

WORK OUT YOUR 'WHY', AND IT'S NOT WORK.

THIS IS A BIG ONE, AND IT'S AT THE HEART OF EVERYTHING I DO.

In business, leadership teams don't usually sit around boardrooms discussing the meaning of life. Year-on-year growth, revenue streams, the bottom line, diversification and risk mitigation are the drivers that steer successful organisations. Now, we're adding recovery to that list.

A company's 'why' will be vastly different to your personal 'why'. Finding synergy always makes for a happy marriage, especially now that you're bringing work into the sanctity of your private space. This is a huge consideration for both businesses and the workforce.

Think about your purpose in relation to that of the company. **Mindset is everything.** If you're not quite in alignment with the 'why' of the organisation you work with, then shift your thinking just enough to feel good about the work you're contributing. Work with heart, always.

Now, let's talk about your individual 'why'.
Sure, you need to generate income so you can pay bills, have security and survive – these are the practical 'why's, the necessities. Beyond your financial needs, the big question is – why are you here?

For me, figuring out my purpose brought me into alignment with my entire universe. **Why am I here? To ignite human potential.** Those four words continue to drive every thought and action I create, from the time I wake up to when I fall asleep at night. It's my daily manifesto.

Being at the helm of a global, multi-platform media business for the past seven years has seen us interview well over 6,000 businesses and individuals. You know what? The majority of them, when asked about their 'why', don't really know what they stand for.

They're so focused on the sale that they can't articulate their 'why'. They can talk for hours underwater about all the product attributes and what makes them so fabulous. This is good too, but the 'why' is the secret ingredient that many of them are missing. If someone doesn't know why they're doing something, is that going to convince you to purchase their product or service or follow their advice? Probably not.

> **There is no greater gift you can give or receive than to honour your calling. It's why you were born and how you become most truly alive.**

– OPRAH WINFREY

It's not complex. In fact, it's very simple.

This is where we get it wrong so often. We get so attached to the specific delivery mechanism, the logistics of how to get it out into the world, that we don't stop to think about why we're doing what we're doing.

When I launched *Collective Hub* in March of 2013, it really didn't matter if it was a print magazine, if I was doing a speaking gig, writing a book or running an online course or a myriad of other things – what mattered was that it aligned with my purpose.

When you know what your purpose is in every single cell of your body, the synchronicity and the serendipity of what you attract will suddenly get into flow and is like nothing you've ever experienced before.

When you find your purpose and step into it, absolutely unbelievable things can happen.

I often throw this challenge out to people – and this is the reason I largely started *Collective Hub* in the first place.

I say, "Let's just agree it's a great product. No question. Now, let's move that aside. What I'm truly interested in is what's your 'why'.

**WHAT DO YOU STAND FOR IN THE WORLD?
WHAT GIVES YOU MEANING?
WHAT'S YOUR STORY BEHIND THE STORY?**

Give it to me – the grit, the raw, the real, the relatable and the attainable."

Once I know you and what you stand for, then I will fall in love with you. Your brand will mean more to me, and will more than likely become a lovemark in my mind, because I know what you stand for and I know that you do too. I bet you can also relate to this.

Don't be shy in bringing what you have to offer the world all the way to the front. You don't just have to show the world the bright shiny thing that's on the outside – there's no feeling in that. **Show me all of you and all of your product. That's where the power is.**

Find your 'why' and you'll never have to work. Instead, you'll play hard with purpose.

Post-COVID-19, the world and the way it 'worked' changed.

It broke. Sometimes when we break things, there is no other option than to reinvent. The business world will have its sleeves rolled up for a very long time reinventing every working part.

How are you going to reinvent – as an intrapreneur, as a corporate leader, as a solopreneur, or as someone who took a direct hit from that curve ball and lost their job?

That is brutal, and the tragic consequence for thousands who are unemployed as a result of this pandemic. If that is you, give yourself a big pat on the back for the great contributions you made to your company. Then give yourself a standing ovation for being here, right now, reading this book, seeking, searching and growing into your new skin.

Like big business, you are literally in the process of reinventing yourself and creating the working life that will bring you closer to your purpose. Unexpected, uninvited change hurts.

HOW DO YOU EVEN BEGIN TO FIND THE BLESSINGS?

Before we get to the hardcore 'how', I want to reiterate that there's wisdom in the 'whys' (get it?!).

> Be brave enough to live the life of your dreams according to your vision and purpose instead of the expectations and opinions of others.

— ROY T. BENNETT

take note

Understand one hundred percent what your purpose is, what you stand for and what you want to put out into the world – but be unattached to the specific delivery mechanism.

ASK YOURSELF:
WHAT WILL IGNITE YOUR POTENTIAL?

There was a time before your last role, and before the role before that, when you had an inner calling that tugged at you to come and play. Like a petulant child it bothered you, pestered you and screamed for your attention until it eventually got bored and ran away.

Whether you were busy in love, busy buying things, or you suddenly had two kids to feed and a mortgage, somehow your 'why' faded away.

It happened to me, only it was my genius who was constantly calling in sick. Eventually, **my 'why' lost interest when I wouldn't play with it.**

Now, you get to be the architect of your new working life.

You're designing the aesthetics, the ergonomics, how you work, when you work best and what muted talents you can now give voice to so you can **pursue your soul's work.**

I believe with all of my heart that finding our purpose is the key to life.

When you find your purpose – your 'why' – everything seems to fall into place and you have a clear mantra to guide you at all times, through all decisions. Which opportunities you should take and what dreams you should chase become much clearer.

All you have to ask yourself is – does this align with my purpose?

> *Be* FEARLESSLY, *authentically you.*
> *No one can hold you back if you're*
> CLEAR *on your purpose.*
> *Stay* TRUE *to* YOURSELF.

@LISA MESSENGER

BE
FEAR
LESS.
BE AU
THENTIC

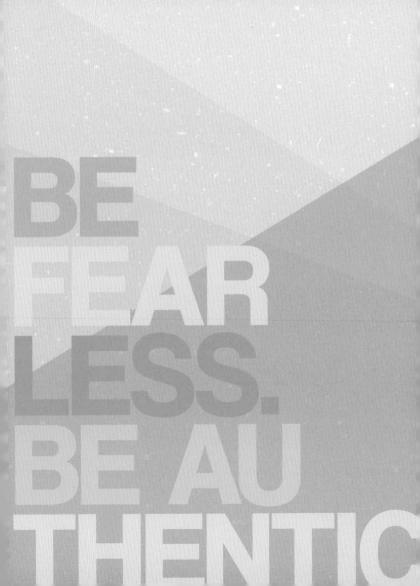

"

Because true belonging only happens when we present our authentic, imperfect selves to the world,

our sense of belonging
can never be greater
than our level of
self-acceptance.

"

– BRENÉ BROWN

2 PLAY

NOW IT'S TIME TO REALLY ASK YOURSELF 'WHY?'.

MY PERSONAL WHY

What am I here to experience?
_____
_____

What am I here to become?
_____
_____

What am I here to give?
_____
_____

What am I here to DO?
_____
_____

When do I feel most ALIVE?
_____
_____

MY BUSINESS WHY

What am I here to achieve?
_____
_____

What am I here to create?
_____
_____

What are my reasons:

Intellectually?
_____

Emotionally?
_____

Spiritually?
_____

Financially?
_____

Now create one sentence that synthesises all of that into one simple directive.

How does your personal 'why' and your business 'why' overlay and intersect?

How can you make it all work for you so that you truly are living your best life AND doing the best you can for your company?

"I am here to..."

_____
_____
_____
_____
_____
_____
_____

This is your personal mission statement.
It will be your spiritual compass and your filter for every decision you make.

YOU...are rebranding.

Notes/comments/takeaways/ideas:

THERE'S WISDOM IN THE WHYS.

@LISAMESSENGER

chapter three

BLAZING A TRAIL

THE AGE OF THE DIGITAL NOMAD SAW TRAILBLAZERS PUT THEIR 'OUT OF OFFICE' ON AND HIT THE SUPER HIGHWAY OF LIFE.

Entrepreneurs, freelancers, solopreneurs, you name it – these changemakers were rejecting the desk and four walls and taking their workstations wherever they desired.

Mostly, the reason was lifestyle choices – to live a life of purpose, freedom and travel as they worked a very different path to the status quo. They knew that they didn't have to choose between their freedom and working – they could build the life they desired and have both.

Sometimes it was a crisis of self or a life crisis such as redundancy, loss of a loved one, or ill health. Whatever the reason, the result was always a **better, freer, more purposeful** work/life blend.

During this digital nomad age, we saw coworking spaces start to spring up, cafes with easy-access power points and community tables set up for people to come in and work from their laptops. People were travelling to the other side of the world all the while running their own business from their laptops. They were truly, working from wherever they were, in that moment.

This was all before COVID-19 of course, but from crisis, catastrophe and chaos, we create change for the better.

Post-pandemic, this is where our headspace needs to be – **seizing the opportunities** and setting up new ways of working.

Together, we will blaze this trail!

> "Use chaos and catastrophe to create change. Re-imagine, pivot and come back stronger than ever before."

@COLLECTIVEHUB

CASE STUDY

Rebel Black

FOUNDER OF THE RURAL WOMAN

Our culture has created a corporate workforce that is often so micromanaged, cluttered, manic, noisy and over-scheduled, and there's very little flexibility outside of the rigid Monday to Friday, nine to five routine.

It's enough to send a free-thinker packing.

The bustling central business district in the heart of a major city isn't the only breeding ground to seed a start-up.

Technology means that we have everything at our fingertips to work and run a business wherever we are. However, so much of the workforce is still caught up in the way we learned to carry out work during the industrial revolution.

Armed with a laptop, a purpose and a passion, Rebel Black decided to blaze a rural trail from her remote office in Lightning Ridge.

Thus, **THE Rural Woman** was born, an online community connecting women who live in rural towns across Australia.

Her 'why'? She wanted to foster innovation, nurture new enterprise and build resilience in rural women around the world.

That's a big vision and a niche opportunity – a rock-solid purpose!

The hashtag '**#bloomwhereyouare**', the catchphrase of THE Rural Woman, now has a digital reach of 50,000 per month, connecting women everywhere online.

I love this case study so much because it not only shows us how **opportunities are literally all around us waiting to be plucked**, but it also teaches us about isolation and connectivity.

I actually grew up in a very rural town named Coolah, on a 4,500 acre property in the middle of nowhere. Sydney was a seven-hour drive away. This was a time before technology, and there weren't the opportunities that exist now for location freedom, so geography absolutely was prohibitive.

In 2018, I purposefully made it my mission to tour 10 towns in 10 days in New South Wales, and 11 towns in 10 days in Queensland, to reach and connect with business owners in rural towns.

I was absolutely blown away by the innovation, creativity and some of the world-class businesses and thought leaders coming out of these remote places.

I personally thrive in isolation because I'm so much more productive when I can power through projects with zero distractions. It wasn't until I left the full-time office environment that **I truly realised the very real difference between being 'busy' and being productive.**

Others struggle with isolation, and that's one of the major hurdles for the newly remote workforce.

Through THE Rural Woman network, Rebel brought the isolated together and made them a community.

Where thousands of kilometres had once kept hundreds of vibrant women feeling alone and completely isolated, they now belonged, connecting, collaborating and supporting each other's business ventures.

What we can learn from this example is how to address emotional isolation when a workforce is very suddenly decentralised. **It's a massive change.**

No more social interactions, no more Nerf wars at knock-off, no kitchen catch ups and no Friday afternoon drinks at the pub across the road. For some, these are the main reasons to show up for work!

The question is, how do you move the team without losing the team spirit? Zoom in.

For an old-school face-to-face, Zoom video conferencing is it, now with an added layer of security for organisations.

Step 1 – create your Zoom account.
Step 2 – check your teeth for spinach.

It's the same rules as in the real world, only you can totally get away with having garlic prawns for lunch before your meeting.

Winner winner eat whatever you want for dinner (but still check your teeth for spinach)!

We touched on **WorkChat** and **WorkPlace** earlier. These are great to hook in groups for work stuff, socialising and virtual events that help build culture.

There are literally hundreds of new technologies launching every day, so watch this space. I'll share more technological tools later on, but for now, I want to show you how to bring play into the day, so your team still feels like just that – a team.

REMEMBER OUR FACEBOOK HQ CASE STUDY?

This is what they did to keep teams and culture thriving. They curated shared Spotify playlists which brought people together through music, shared podcasts, books and e-courses, hopped on fitness apps together and created watch parties for their favourite Facebook watch shows.

My amazing friend Jacquie shared a recent story of their Global Sales and Marketing Conference that brings together 10, 000 Facebook staff from around the globe every year for three days of incredible content. Facebook team members love this event.

Two weeks out when it had to be cancelled due to COVID-19, **what did Facebook HQ do?** They pivoted and came up with the **'Un-summit'.**

Content was created, fast and furious production flooded in and ideas flourished, making it a bigger, better, and truly global event that people absolutely loved and blew up their Instagram.

> *Sometimes the BEST things in life are UNEXPECTED.*
>
> – FAITH SULLIVAN

"

Permanence, perseverance and persistence in spite of all obstacles, discouragements, and impossibilities:

**It is this,
that in all things
distinguishes
the strong soul
from the weak.**

"

– THOMAS CARLYLE

take note

FOR FOUNDERS AND CEOS

Decentralising your team is the perfect time to reinstate your company vision and remind people what you are all working towards. At the same time, allow employees to overlay that with their current reality and how they need their life to look right now. Remember, allowing someone to feel heard is the strongest measure of support.

BLAZE YOUR TRAIL AND GET IN THE GAME

@LISAMESSENGER

3
PLAY

USE YOUR TECH TO STAY CONNECTED.

Research companies that are using technology to stay connected.

What are the top initiatives you've come across that you hadn't previously thought of?

1. _____
2. _____
3. _____
4. _____
5. _____

How could these newly found initiatives work for you?

_____
_____
_____
_____
_____
_____

List some tech that you **used** to use to stay connected:

1. _____
2. _____
3. _____
4. _____
5. _____

List some new tech that you have discovered while being impacted by COVID-19:

1. _____
2. _____
3. _____
4. _____
5. _____

How have these new ways of connecting brought you together with people in your network, both in personal life and your career?

_____
_____
_____
_____

> **Coming together is a beginning, staying together is progress, and working together is success.**

– HENRY FORD

Notes/comments/takeaways/ideas:

embrace
change

move on
& thrive

chapter four

FLIP FEAR

OVERCOMING FEAR AND SELF-SABOTAGE.

THERE CAN BE A LOT OF NEGATIVE CONNOTATIONS AROUND FEAR, HOWEVER IT DOES HAVE A ROLE. ITS PURPOSE IS TO KEEP US ALIVE.

Without it, we would fearlessly plunge to our deaths before we turned 10. Fear of heights, fear of dangerous animals, fear of putting our hand into that pot of boiling water, fear of walking alone through the park at midnight – we can thank these fears for keeping us safe.

The trick with fear, however, is that we often fear the fear itself.

I'm sure you're familiar with this situation – you have this brand new idea that you think would make a great business, podcast, blog or book. You think about it for days on end, but there's something that keeps you hesitant about doing anything about it.

There's that little voice telling you to stay comfortable and not take the leap, because hundreds of things could go wrong and put you in uncomfortable and challenging situations.

Ultimately, we decide to let the idea go. That is our fear of fear that ultimately results in self-sabotage, and it's a pattern that has to end. **We just can't let it bully us into believing we're going to fail.**

As with any bully, you have to look it squarely in the eye and show it who's boss.

Easier said than done when we've just experienced an unprecedented global fail. Uncertainty is the only thing we can be certain about when a once-in-a-hundred-year event hits us.

We can't control the uncontrollable, and fear of the unknown is the most common fear shared amongst humans. We become paralysed, scared that whatever we do next isn't going to be the right thing because we don't know what tomorrow is going to look like.

WHAT DO WE DO ABOUT IT?

We choose to give fear the flip.

Nothing sound or strategic ever comes from a place of fight or flight. However, we can listen calmly to what fear has to say and use it to mitigate risk, prepare and plan and, if projections are reliable, to prosper.

Remember our case study on Rebel Black back in chapter three (page 102)? I love Rebel's story so much, and I think part of this is because even her name tells fear where it can go – it's literally Rebel.

Calmly, Rebel moved through each stage of her business plan, creating solutions to problems and finding new pathways armed with a belief she could build a viable and successful business working remotely.

HOW DO WE OVERCOME FEAR AND SELF-SABOTAGE?

There's so much value in building connections and sharing what you know, so my first tip is to always ask questions.

When I launched *Collective Hub*, one of my biggest challenges was a highly saturated market (there were about 5,500 print magazines in Australia alone) which people said was either "dead" or "dying". That may well have been the case, but **when you have a strong idea, a big vision and unwavering self-belief, anything is possible,** no matter how saturated the market or how dire a perceived situation is.

As is well documented now, my idea flew. Within eighteen months, the print magazine was in 37 countries. I believed in myself and knew that there was a need for it.

People want a **sense of belonging** and to feel like they're part of something bigger than themselves, and when they're given that, they will take your purpose and spread it far and wide.

Our *Collective Hub* community largely carried the message for me, and the rest is history. People were used to just hearing part of the story, but I wanted to tell the whole story – the story behind the story, the how, the why, the raw, the real, the relatable and attainable, about brilliant businesses and individuals traversing industry sectors and geographic locations.

The *Collective Hub* story is so pertinent today when many of us find ourselves fearful, unsure of what's next and physically disconnected from others.

None of that stopped me in 2013. My team and I reached people all over the globe through our print, digital and event platforms. It was all about **connection and humanising** the experience, no matter where anyone was located.

LET'S BREAK THAT DOWN.

Collective Hub's early barriers were that:

- It was going to cost me over $350,000 to launch with the first issue.

- People didn't take me seriously because I had no experience

- Print was said to be dead or dying.

- I knew nothing about the supply chain or how to distribute a magazine.

- Being based in Australia, initially people didn't take me seriously on a world stage.

- I knew nothing at the time about the online space and how to digitise our offering.

- I lacked skills to build a website, landing page, had limited technology know-how and knew nothing of the social-sphere.

- There were limited financial resources to hand over and outsource.

> **Obstacles don't have to stop you. If you run into a wall, don't turn around and give up.**

> Figure out how
> to climb it,
> go through it,
> or work around it.

— MICHAEL JORDAN

All that being said, it was still absolutely doable. I knew that what I didn't know or didn't have the skills for, someone on my team would, or we would find where to learn what we needed to.

Once I broke it down, I systematically addressed each challenge through **disciplined, methodical work with a small team of three and stuck with the process.**

When we look at the big picture, the combined fears can make it seem super daunting and, often, so much so that we don't start at all.

Our small team just put one foot in front of the other, working on the next logical thing. Sometimes, naivety can be a good thing. In this case, it worked in our favour. We didn't know what we didn't know, so we were unafraid.

Collective Hub went on to be one of the greatest launches in Australian media history. We went on to diversify and pivot into a serious digital content and ecommerce business, despite everything being stacked against us.

That's how I know, for sure, that when you truly believe in yourself, you can achieve the impossible, even in the hardest and most turbulent of times.

take note

When fear comes up when you're faced with a huge task, project or problem, break it down into much smaller challenges and just work through solving one small challenge at a time.

@LISAMESSENGER

WHERE WAS FEAR THROUGHOUT THIS?

It was disempowered, cowering in the corner having a crisis. We were building what it hates most – knowledge. **Fear had no place to fester.**

That's my second tip when it comes to fear – arm yourself with knowledge.

In this day and age, we have more access to knowledge than we ever have before. Training, mentoring programs, coaching, YouTube tutorials, media publications, networking groups, collaborators, platforms, apps, masterclasses and infinite short and long courses are all available to us online at any time. You already have your head in the game because you're here right now, gaining knowledge and growing.

You are literally a magnet for learning, an undergraduate in this digital universe of knowledge. The Internet stores the answers to pretty much every question we could ever think to ask because it's contributed to by literally every person in society – and that's just one tool.

Having access to the online world means that we have access to information from billions of human brains around the world who are all uploading their information.

take note

Speaking of knowledge, help yourself or your team members by upskilling whilst working from home. There's a myriad of incredible online courses that can help your teams feel like they have momentum and are moving forward.

@LISAMESSENGER

When we're faced with having to immediately upskill to meet a demand, we may become overwhelmed. Sometimes time is against us, and trawling the Internet to find instant answers can be frustrating. This is a message to all the bosses reading this – get the systems and technology in place, fast.

What we as individuals can do to feel more in control is tuck a metaphorical pocket book of knowledge into our back pockets. Search all possible rabbit holes for information sources pertinent to your business sector. The beautiful thing is there are so many channels out there that we'd need an entire book, and that book would change daily.

I love this quote from my inspiring, thought-leader friend, Marie Forleo:

"Transform panic into preparedness."

Absolute gold.

By compiling your super bank of data and updating it along the way, you'll have help on demand. Sudden problems can easily be turned into solutions because now you'll know where to go to get the knowledge you need to meet that challenge head-on.

MAINTAINING RESILIENCE IN THE FACE OF FEAR

If you know me, you know that I live my life out loud and use myself as a conduit to go through challenges and then give you all the lessons I learn along the way. I have faced quite a lot of adversity and challenges in my journey so far, and I predict there are still a lot more ahead of me.

These challenges have caused me to have to pivot over and over again, and I have built up a lot of resilience as a result.

I think **resilience is important when we talk about fear.** The more we build resilience, the less chance our fear has to control the situation, because our resilience is there in its spot at the wheel. The more challenging situations we work our way through and the more we pivot, the more we're building and strengthening that resilience muscle.

As much as COVID-19 has displaced us and caused mass amounts of loss, it has also required us to be more resilient than we've possibly ever had to be before.

Resilience builds that knowledge of how to overcome adversity, and as we know, knowledge is fear's enemy. It means that the next time you're faced with a tough situation, you'll have the tools, knowledge and resources to know how to face it, and fear won't be able to stick around much longer.

With resilience, you'll know that you can keep putting one foot in front of the other.

Flip fear, and flip stress while we're at it, too. It's time to be prepared and get productivity levels back to business as usual.

❝

Don't FEAR *failure so much that you* REFUSE *to try new things. The* SADDEST *summary of a life contains three descriptions:* COULD *have,* MIGHT *have, and* SHOULD *have.*

– LOUIS E. BOONE

❞

PREPARATION PREVENTS PAIN

@LISAMESSENGER

4
PLAY

IT'S TIME TO TOSS FEAR AND SELF-SABOTAGE AWAY AND NEVER LOOK BACK!

Firstly, let's overcome some of that fear with a few simple steps to provide some perspective:

What are you worrying about right now?

___
___
___
___
___

Will it matter ten minutes from now?

___
___

Will it matter ten months from now?

___
___

Will it matter ten years from now?
_____
_____

Will it matter ten decades from now?
_____
_____

What's the worst case scenario? Provide some detail:
_____
_____
_____
_____
_____
_____
_____
_____
_____
_____
_____

Think of a previous situation that you felt was as dire as this one. I take it you survived it as you're reading this now.

What did you do and who did you rely on to get through it? Write about it here:

_____
_____
_____
_____
_____
_____
_____
_____
_____
_____
_____
_____
_____
_____

There – feel better now? You've got this!

Notes/comments/takeaways/ideas:

"

Each of us must confront our own fears, must come face to face with them.

How we handle our fears will determine where we go with the rest of our lives.

To experience adventure or to be limited by the fear of it."
"

– JUDY BLUME

chapter five

THE LOGISTICS

NAILING THE LOGISTIC HOW-TOS

NOW THAT YOU HAVE YOUR 'WHY' AND YOUR HEAD IS IN THE NOW, IT'S TIME TO GET INTO THE LOGISTICS.

Working from home wouldn't be possible without our blessed Internet. Sometimes, though, it really can be a love/hate relationship.

We all know what it's like to be home, ready to chill in front of the TV with a bowl of popcorn at the end of a long day, when apparently everyone else in your building has the same idea. Enter the spinning wheel of death.

Sharing the home with family, housemates and pets adds extra layers of difficulty to navigating your best and most productive work day. You have the kids streaming a movie or flatmates playing Minecraft while you're trying to upload a document, and suddenly it's dropping out and failing. Then, your hangry cat stomps across your keyboard trying to get your attention.

The struggle is real.

Shifting all of the responsibility to the worker isn't reasonable, so make sure that you have discussions with everyone on your team about how to handle the operating side of things, such as storage and the ensuing avalanche of daily hits to their inbox.

You need to do everything you can to ease the strain while the team finds their feet.

Solopreneur, entrepreneur, departmental manager leading the team…whatever your role, everyone needs to feel that they have the correct working tools so they can do just that – work. If not, this will only lead to technical issues, more stress and less productive work.

There are certain basics that we all need. One is a reliable, high-speed Internet connection. Then you need capacity and web security – cyber attacks can be costly and disruptive for both the company and you personally.

If workers have to use their own hardware and home networks, these might lack the built-in safety tools of business networks, such as custom-built firewalls, serious antivirus software and online automatic back-ups.

Without these security measures there's **increased risk of malware**, putting sensitive personal and work information at risk.

If you are being left to your own devices or you're a solopreneur, thankfully there are a few basic things you can do to ramp up security.

SOME QUICK TIPS TO GET YOU CYBER-READY:

- Use a really strong password. I know, this seems a bit obvious. However, sometimes in the chaos of moving house, someone leaves the key in the front door, so we must always remember to lock up.

- Set up two-factor authentication, firewalls and antivirus software.

COVID-19 has shown us how vulnerable we are to surprise attacks, so immunise your setup from computer viruses that could bring your operation to its knees.

You probably have some sort of built-in firewall, so check that it's enabled. If you don't have strong enough protection, free options like **ZoneAlarm, Free Firewall** and **AVS** are worth looking into.

A good firewall is vital, but threats can still get through, so antivirus gear is your next line of defence as it can detect and block known malware. **Norton, McAfee** and **Bitdefender** are really good options.

Remember, you don't have the might of your company's big software so you need to protect your information from what's out there.

SECURITY TIPS FOR WORKING SAFELY FROM HOME:

- Use a Virtual Private Network (VPN). This encrypts all of your Internet traffic so it's unreadable to hackers. A downside, however, is that it can slow down Internet speeds, so video conferencing calls and anything performing high-bandwidth tasks will be frustrating at best. You might consider upgrading to Express VPN which can handle it. Perimeter 81 and ScribeForce are also worth a quick Google search.

- If you're like me and technology talk just makes your eyes glaze over, compareitech.com is a great resource for this stuff. You don't have to get it, you just have to get the system that best protects you.

There are complexities, so do everything possible to facilitate a happy move, whether you're flying solo or flying the whole team. You want to make sure you have a safe landing. Everyone needs to feel 100 percent supported, then productivity can rocket back to the new normal. That's our end game.

YOUR WORK SPACE

Now that you get to work from home, it's time to set up the ultimate work space. While you don't want your home looking like the office, you also can't curl up on the couch like a slug and expect to be productive.

It's worth it to spend some time and money getting your space right, because if you're going to hit it, it's so much easier when you love where you physically work. Home is our happy place, and we want to build on that and create a dedicated happy space for working.

Make it look good and feel good.

Get the right chair to support your back, ensure the lighting is functional and everything works. You might like to work with lots of desk supplies like sticky notes and folders, or you may prefer a minimalist desk set-up.

Whatever your preference, the exciting part is that it's up to you now.

It's your home, and your life, so think outside the cubicle – you're the architect now. How amazing that now, every work day, you get to spend it in your happy space.

NOW, TO AN IMPORTANT QUESTION – SHOULD I WEAR PANTS?

It's 7am on a Monday morning. It's raining outside and you don't want to get out of your perfectly comfortable, cozy bed, but you can't miss your 9am meeting.

This sounds like a recipe for a day off, but **you don't want to be that person.**

Freelancers, sole traders, solopreneurs – you're already the boss of you. If you're not accountable for your own productivity, work ethic and level of commitment, that's your problem. You guys get a free pass from this part of the book, so go and grab yourselves a creative break. Or, stick around for the fun of it!

some fun

Back to those boundaries we were talking about earlier with mental health – creating a work space in your home will help with this. When you have a designated spot for work that you don't spend time in when you're not working, it can really help separate work time from time to just relax and chill out.

@LISAMESSENGER

Managers, I'm speaking to you right now. Your team is geographically all over the place.

HOW DO YOU KEEP THEM ENGAGED, PRODUCTIVE AND ACCOUNTABLE WHEN YOU'RE NOT THERE TO PHYSICALLY OVERSEE THEM?

You don't want a tight and talented workforce to splinter into a disenfranchised work-mob that's all over the place and not performing.

First, let's head back to isolation. We touched on this earlier – it's good to empathise with everyone's experience of suddenly being amputated from their own collective hub. It's a huge psychological shift for workers who are part of a social and buzzing hive of activity. If not handled with care, working from home can feel like solitary confinement, so we need to acknowledge the emotions that go with that.

Rest assured most of your team are probably going through the same experiences, emotions and feelings.

I know the entrepreneurs out there are saying, "Isolation? Awesome. I can get way more done. I love isolation!"

At the same time, I bet there are just as many workers out there who are struggling to come to terms with the new way of working after being so used to working in an office for years and years, if not decades.

It's important to acknowledge that we're all coming at it from a completely different headspace. We actually need to engage our heartspace, **connect and collaborate.**

It's crucial to encourage new and playful ways to keep your team socially connected so we're not leaving anyone behind.

A few ideas are to send an invite for Friday knock-off drinks on a **Zoom** call, gamify a team project or encourage social hangouts on video sharing platforms.

You might also like to encourage everyone to send a group email or message when they're celebrating something awesome that the office would normally celebrate, so you still keep that sense of collective achievement and joy.

This sort of connection isn't time wasting. It's team building.

When team members feel socially connected with the fun stuff and are seen and valued for more than just their output, they'll find it so much easier to plug into work hangouts and get the job done.

BE INVENTIVE AND ENABLE THE CONNECTIONS THAT BUILD A SENSE OF BELONGING.

THAT'S WHEN TEAMS WORK.

@LISAMESSENGER

If you allow play to live across your team's work day, you'll stitch the culture back together and have a full squad of team players. It's so easy to get caught up in hitting the keyboard for ten hours a day and expecting everyone else in the team to do the same in the name of efficiency.

However, we know enough about burnout and stress to know that this isn't actually efficient, and time spent focused on building connection is one of the **most valuable** business investments you will ever make.

Not only that – isolation and loneliness are the most frequent challenges I hear from people who have recently made the transition to working from home. This was heightened even more when we were all living in lockdown when the pandemic first hit and we couldn't meet up with friends or family either.

If you're in charge of a team, the best thing you can do for the mental health of the entire team (including yourself!) is to prioritise and schedule moments for connecting with one another throughout the week.

Now, let's get some systems in place to help keep everyone accountable.

OPERATIONAL TOOLS

Team check-ins. I set up daily 'pulse checks' for my team, checking in with all the hearts that make up *Collective Hub*. We all have location freedom, meaning we work from wherever, whenever, so these check-ins help us all get a handle on what's happening and where everyone is at. They also cultivate a positive culture where the team feels heard and seen, and we can talk through things together.

Asana. Asana is a project management tool that serves as a collaborative to-do list for everyone on your team. You can map out all the tasks of an entire project and assign different tasks to different people, chat about tasks with team members and also use it as your personal to-do list. I love Asana for mapping out and keeping track of projects, as well as keeping tabs of what everyone has on their plate.

Slack. What are the budgets? What meetings have we got coming up? What are the timelines, reporting and KPIs? We also have a constant Slack chat going on so no one ever feels like they're not part of the conversation. If you're not familiar with Slack, it's an instant messaging platform for teams that syncs across everyone's devices, reducing the need for constant meetings because we can share information, collaborate and come together instantly and on-the-go. Slack keeps us all in-touch and up-to-date with what's going on.

word of advice

Relax policies and guidelines to display empathy and flexibility. Understand that many people will still be adjusting to working from home, but often with kids and partners in the mix. Work to their schedule where possible and remain nimble. Try to focus on output, KPIs and productivity, rather than on specific hours. Now more than ever, data is our friend in enabling people to be trusted and work to their schedules. In order to keep the now of work, we need to show that we trust everyone on our teams and respect their own individual lives and schedules.

@LISAMESSENGER

Our team has been working this way since 2018, so by now we have it running like clockwork. However, something important to keep in mind is that **there are new technologies emerging every day**, and we never stop learning, adapting and introducing new ways of doing things to improve the way we work.

Once you successfully untether from a centralised work environment, speaking from experience, there's no going back.

It's freedom, it's efficient and it works. You'll see that there is absolutely no need to go back to an office space that is only sucking money from the business.

Fast forward to **the now of work**, you've got so many tricks and tools at your disposal to leave the ball and chain of old-school working behind you. In years to come, it might even seem that the yesterday of work was the disease, and COVID-19 the brutal cure.

We didn't want it to happen this way.

No one wants extreme pain on a scale this unimaginable and this devastating to the economy, our businesses and our precious way of life. If we have to swallow such a bitter pill, then we owe it to ourselves to get well soon and create an even healthier way of working and living going forward.

WHAT IS OUR WORK HERE?

All of our job descriptions now include something universally greater than any one role. United, we embrace the leap that has moved enterprise to the home space.

We need to energise our work teams with innovative leadership that inspires. Make everyone feel part of something meaningful, something bigger, as you together reinvent the company, reinvigorate your brand and zoom in on the big picture. The universe has sent us a pretty obvious sign that something wasn't working. **Now, it's time to revolutionise work for everyone.**

OH, AND TO ANSWER YOUR EARLIER QUESTION – YES, IT'S A GOOD IDEA TO WEAR PANTS!

"Zoom might reveal something nobody needs to see!"

This subject line of a direct message from my inspiring friend, Turia Pitt, caused a collective, loud laugh from my entire team.

We love Turia's unstoppable spirit. If there's an Australian who can teach us resilience, empowerment and true bloody grit, it's Turia. She finds the light and the play in everything and does it with real character.

> Because of what I've been through I know that I can get through hard times and I know that I'm capable of anything I put my mind to. That's what tough times teach us. Each time I go through a tough time in my life now, I think 'I've had tough times before, and I've survived them – I'm gonna survive this one too'.

– TURIA PITT

The tragedy of COVID-19 will reward companies who lead with the same tenacity of spirit.

The virus has tested, and will continue to test, a company's values to the core as we recalibrate and grow our way out of this, and not just in the fiscal sense.

I'm talking in a human sense as we re-evaluate how we actually do business.

Chairman and Managing Director of Konica Minolta, Dr David Cooke, is my inspiring friend and an innovative thinker.

I admire him so much for his heart-driven leadership.

We caught up to talk about how his company has adapted to moving to remote work.

Let's break down how Konica Minolta pivoted with purpose.

CASE STUDY
Konica Minolta

As well as the practical implications of learning to work together in a virtual way, Konica Minolta's priority was to rethink health, safety and wellbeing for the whole team.

Virtual team meetings, drinks and lunches were scheduled to keep people connected.

Microsoft Teams became their tool of choice to create live and on-demand team events with the added benefit of the same enterprise-level security, compliance and management features of Office 365.

Konica Minolta were ahead of the game in terms of having already equipped most of their workforce with remote technologies.

They recognised this transition was what made for happy team members, so when COVID-19 hit, they were halfway there with the right technology, sharing and collaboration platforms in place to just plug in and go.

Konica Minolta acknowledges that digitising processes, optimising workflows and enabling a virtual workforce are now must-haves, not merely 'nice-to-haves'. It was all in place to support a virtual workforce and be connected remotely.

They made sure every member of the team felt **supported and connected**, both spiritually and socially.

These are my favourite companies, led by my favourite leadership teams. **They get it.**

Konica Minolta might be a technology business, but they're a people company. They planned ahead. They were aware there would be additional stresses in the home environment, so their focus was on how to be more considerate and compassionate, all amid change and uncertainty.

This says so much about a company's values.

Whereas once they asked people to bring their whole selves to work, now people's work was in their homes.

They knew there would be pluses – sharing their work day with loved ones, time out with pets – but there were personal stresses for some, and reaching out to ask if people were coping with the transition became a big priority for the managers.

Tech support, training support and personal support all worked to facilitate a smooth and urgent transition for the company. Not only that, but they found the silver linings of moving their team to working remotely.

This year, the Konica Minolta annual kick-off event had to be reimagined. Traditionally, only 300 sales executives and management were invited to an event that celebrated the company's successes. Now, it's become an online event to include the **entire company.**

Out of physical isolation came something much bigger. An opportunity for everyone to be involved, interact and ask questions of the senior executive team.

What a fantastic share of logistics and humanity.

STAY CONNECTED AND MEET PEOPLE WHERE **THEY** ARE.

@LISAMESSENGER

WHAT DOES WORKING FROM HOME LOOK LIKE FOR YOU AND YOUR TEAM?

It's such an exciting leap.

Working this way can actually empower the team. With great, innovative leadership, they can feel more engaged, more inspired, more supported and super fired up to embrace the change forced upon this workforce of now. They themselves will be part of this worldwide shift.

We're all in this together. We're all accountable for making it better than it was before, for ourselves and the workforce of the future.

Lead with heart, and your team will never just 'dial it in'.

They'll want in because they're buying into a future that takes care of people, the planet and business, and recognises that individuals are so much more than just the hours they clock at the desk.

> We're all in this together. It's okay to be honest. It's okay to ask for help. It's okay to say you're stuck, or that you're haunted or that you can't begin to let go. We can all relate to those things. Screw the stigma that says otherwise. Break the silence and break the cycle, for you are more than just your pain. You are not alone. And people need other people.

– JAMIE TWORKOWSKI

> **CRISES AND DEADLOCKS WHEN THEY OCCUR HAVE AT LEAST THIS ADVANTAGE,**

THAT THEY FORCE US TO THINK.

"

– JAWAHARLAL NEHRU

5
—

PLAY

NOW WE CAN GET PERSONAL WITH YOUR LOGISTICS!

Firstly, **how did you go with setting up your home office space?** Is it a place you love to work? Write down your favourite things about your new working space:

_____
_____
_____
_____

I'd love to see your new inspiring office space! Share some pics with me on Instagram! **@lisamessenger**

What can you do to improve your space a little more? Write down an actionable strategy to make this happen:

_____
_____
_____
_____

HOW HAVE YOU, OR HOW WILL YOU, HANDLE YOUR LOGISTICS THROUGH THIS WORK FROM HOME MOVEMENT?

Where and how will you hold all your meetings? Will they be via a virtual software?

_____
_____

Where will you store all your product and/or physical inventory?

_____
_____

Where will your work mail get sent?

_____
_____

How will you manage KPIs?

_____
_____

What will you do with all your tech, furniture and infrastructure?

_____

_____

Will your team use their own devices or will you supply them? Will they be able to take their work computers and devices home with them?

_____

_____

How will your team brainstorm? What tech will you use to do this?

_____

_____

TIP: You probably have some sort of built-in firewall on your current devices – so check that it's enabled. If you don't have strong enough protection, free options like ZoneAlarm Free Firewall and AVG are worth looking into.

LIST SOME MANAGERS, BOSSES OR CEOS WHO YOU ADMIRE FOR THEIR LEADERSHIP STYLES. RESEARCH THEM AND LEARN ABOUT WHAT 'HEART' DRIVES THEIR 'SMARTS'.

Name:

Why you admire them:
_____
_____

Name:

Why you admire them:
_____
_____

Name:

Why you admire them:
_____
_____

Name:

Why you admire them:
_____
_____

Name:

Why you admire them:
_____
_____

GREAT – NOW THESE PEOPLE ARE YOUR NEW VIRTUAL MENTORS! TAKE THESE LESSONS AND USE THEM TO INSPIRE YOU AND YOUR TEAM. IMPLEMENT THEIR STRATEGIES AND SEE HOW YOUR STAFF OR COLLEAGUES REACT! NOTE SOME CHANGES YOU'VE SEEN HERE:

_____
_____
_____
_____

Notes/comments/takeaways/ideas:

> Show me a successful individual and I'll show you someone who had real positive influences in his or her life. I don't care what you do for a living –

if you do it well I'm sure there was someone cheering you on or showing the way. A mentor.

"

– DENZEL WASHINGTON

chapter six

LOCATION FREEDOM

HACKS TO GET YOU HOME AND HOSED.

THE SAD PART OF A SUDDEN AND SWIFT MOVE TO THE WONDERS OF WORKING FROM HOME IS THAT YOU DIDN'T GET TIME TO STOP AND SMELL THE ROSES.

Instead, it happened overnight in a haze of panic and overwhelm. You didn't get to make the choice of when and how, and you had to adjust to the transition in the midst of a global crisis. It's still DEFCON 3 out there, and that certainly wasn't the plan.

For entrepreneurs, we thrive in a crisis – even one as immense and intense as COVID-19. We work well when there's chaos and unrealistic deadlines. If there's a challenge, you can always count on us to stick our hands right up for it and dig in.

However, that's just one type of person. For others, it's confusing, frightening and utterly overwhelming, **which is completely normal** – we are dealing with a global pandemic and all its ramifications after all.

We all know that **operating from chaos never produces good outcomes**, so let's catch our breath, find our calm, and think like an entrepreneur.

I'm going to ask you to join the dance. Pivot, be flexible, be nimble, bend, stretch and really reach as we problem-solve our way through every unchoreographed step in this unrehearsed ballet.

There's no such thing as a misstep – there's only learning.

From here on in, we are all entrepreneurs, each of us thinking on our feet and creating solutions together.

> NEVER *give up, because you never know if the* NEXT *try is going to be the* ONE *that* WORKS.
>
> – MARY KAY ASH

> We're all in this game together.

— WILLIAM STYRON

CASE STUDY

OZ Design Furniture

OZ Design Furniture is an incredible company, an Australian-owned and operated business selling furniture and homewares. They've been in business for over 40 years and were directly impacted by the social distancing measures imposed due to the pandemic.

Through each stage of the government's emergency plan **they pivoted and put safety and wellbeing first** – for their customers, delivery drivers and staff.

Head Office quickly became a home office. **Zoom** conferencing, **WhatsApp** chat groups and **Skype** all eased the burden of emails.

Efficient communication became absolutely paramount. Amongst the practicals, they took a beat and did something amazing. They penned a new mission statement:

'To recover with greater purpose and meaning.'

I love this.

It shows that behind all the actionables that needed to be taken, there was heart.

Focus fast shifted to their website and online business.

Originally, OZ Design Furniture was built on being a 'see it and try it' in-store model, which customers loved. They now had to transfer that experience across to the digital space, producing video content that would help customers feel comfortable and confident to shop from home.

I proudly became a part of telling this story with a new desk and couch that supplemented my work from home lifestyle so that others could see it being used in action.

This was key. OZ Design Furniture knew it was how they presented to the market, even more than the great product they were selling, that would ultimately get them through.

Their business depended on it.

"

Maybe it did take a crisis to get to know yourself; maybe you needed to get whacked hard by life

before you understood what you wanted out of it.

"

– JODI PICOULT

Think about how you can create brand trust through the messaging you present to your market.

This is where defining your brand 'why' and defining your story serves you so much more than simply going straight to the 'hard sell' on how fantastic your product is.

Just like we're creating the new now of work, it's also time to create the new now of business, which means existing for purpose, keeping that purpose front of mind and at the centre of everything we do, and always communicating to our tribe from the heart.

It's the story behind your story that customers buy into before they consciously buy your product. There's feeling and power in your 'why'. Communicate it unashamedly.

I just love how businesses come together offering insight to help the entire community. It's the best side of any disaster – our human goodness that underpins everything we are.

We've seen it in every disaster before.

People want to help.
We need each other, and that need to band together is only strengthened during challenging times.

OZ DESIGN FURNITURE HAVE SOME REALLY SOLID TIPS FOR BUSINESSES IN THE FACE OF THE GLOBAL PANDEMIC:

- Focus on the areas of your business you have direct control over, such as stock, incoming inventory, advertising or media schedules. These are your controllables, so take stock.

- Be sure to always stay in the positive.

- Show leadership. Your team needs your strong direction.

- Find the opportunity in every challenging situation. There is always one, often many.

In my opinion, these are brilliant tips that can be applied all the time, not just post-COVID-19. In order to keep the now of work after the pandemic is all over, we must keep all the learnings and the new mindset we have cultivated during this time with us.

> It's a funny thing about life, once you begin to take note of the things you are grateful for, you begin to lose sight of the things that you lack.

— GERMANY KENT

WHILE THIS IS FRESH IN YOUR MIND, LET'S DIVE INTO AN EXERCISE TO GET YOUR THOUGHTS INTO THIS SORT OF MINDSET.

USE MY 'WORK FROM HOME' PLANNER ACROSS THE NEXT FEW PAGES TO HELP YOU REMAIN IN CONTROL AND ON TRACK! WE'VE GIVEN YOU FIVE DAYS WORTH TO PLAN RIGHT NOW.

TIP: YOU CAN CUT OUT THESE PAGES AND PHOTOCOPY THEM, SO YOU CAN USE THEM FOREVER!

OR, YOU CAN JUMP ONLINE AND PURCHASE OUR PHYSICAL WORK FROM HOME DESK PLANNER FROM COLLECTIVEHUB.COM

WORK FROM HOME
daily planner

TOP 3 WORK PRIORITIES:

- ○ _____
- ○ _____
- ○ _____

TOP 3 PERSONAL PRIORITIES:

- ○ _____
- ○ _____
- ○ _____

WORK TO-DO LIST:

- ○ _____
- ○ _____
- ○ _____
- ○ _____
- ○ _____
- ○ _____
- ○ _____
- ○ _____
- ○ _____
- ○ _____

PERSONAL TO-DO LIST:

- ○ _____
- ○ _____
- ○ _____
- ○ _____
- ○ _____
- ○ _____
- ○ _____
- ○ _____
- ○ _____
- ○ _____

RESOURCES NEEDED TO SUCCEED:

- ○ _____
- ○ _____
- ○ _____
- ○ _____
- ○ _____

RESOURCES NEEDED TO SUCCEED:

- ○ _____
- ○ _____
- ○ _____
- ○ _____
- ○ _____

ROUTINES AND RITUALS

MORNING ROUTINE:

5am
6am
7am
8am
9am
10am
11am

AFTERNOON ROUTINE:

12pm
1pm
2pm
3pm
4pm
5pm
6pm

EVENING ROUTINE:

7pm
8pm
9pm
10pm
11pm
12am

TODAY'S BEST MOMENT:

DAILY ACHIEVEMENTS

WORK:

PERSONAL:

EXERCISE:

FOOD:

MINDSET:

FUN:

DAILY GRATITUDE:

WORK FROM HOME
daily planner

TOP 3 WORK PRIORITIES:
-
-
-

TOP 3 PERSONAL PRIORITIES:
-
-
-

WORK TO-DO LIST:
-
-
-
-
-
-
-
-
-
-

PERSONAL TO-DO LIST:
-
-
-
-
-
-
-
-
-
-

RESOURCES NEEDED TO SUCCEED:
-
-
-
-
-

RESOURCES NEEDED TO SUCCEED:
-
-
-
-
-

ROUTINES AND RITUALS

MORNING ROUTINE:

5am
6am
7am
8am
9am
10am
11am

AFTERNOON ROUTINE:

12pm
1pm
2pm
3pm
4pm
5pm
6pm

EVENING ROUTINE:

7pm
8pm
9pm
10pm
11pm
12am

TODAY'S BEST MOMENT:

DAILY ACHIEVEMENTS

WORK:

PERSONAL:

EXERCISE:

FOOD:

MINDSET:

FUN:

DAILY GRATITUDE:

WORK FROM HOME
daily planner

TOP 3 WORK PRIORITIES:
- ○ _____
- ○ _____
- ○ _____

TOP 3 PERSONAL PRIORITIES:
- ○ _____
- ○ _____
- ○ _____

WORK TO-DO LIST:
- ○ _____
- ○ _____
- ○ _____
- ○ _____
- ○ _____
- ○ _____
- ○ _____
- ○ _____
- ○ _____
- ○ _____

PERSONAL TO-DO LIST:
- ○ _____
- ○ _____
- ○ _____
- ○ _____
- ○ _____
- ○ _____
- ○ _____
- ○ _____
- ○ _____
- ○ _____

RESOURCES NEEDED TO SUCCEED:
- ○ _____
- ○ _____
- ○ _____
- ○ _____
- ○ _____

RESOURCES NEEDED TO SUCCEED:
- ○ _____
- ○ _____
- ○ _____
- ○ _____
- ○ _____

ROUTINES AND RITUALS

MORNING ROUTINE:

5am
6am
7am
8am
9am
10am
11am

AFTERNOON ROUTINE:

12pm
1pm
2pm
3pm
4pm
5pm
6pm

EVENING ROUTINE:

7pm
8pm
9pm
10pm
11pm
12am

TODAY'S BEST MOMENT:

DAILY ACHIEVEMENTS

WORK:

PERSONAL:

EXERCISE:

FOOD:

MINDSET:

FUN:

DAILY GRATITUDE:

WORK FROM HOME
daily planner

TOP 3 WORK PRIORITIES:
- ___
- ___
- ___

TOP 3 PERSONAL PRIORITIES:
- ___
- ___
- ___

WORK TO-DO LIST:
- ___
- ___
- ___
- ___
- ___
- ___
- ___
- ___
- ___
- ___

PERSONAL TO-DO LIST:
- ___
- ___
- ___
- ___
- ___
- ___
- ___
- ___
- ___
- ___

RESOURCES NEEDED TO SUCCEED:
- ___
- ___
- ___
- ___
- ___

RESOURCES NEEDED TO SUCCEED:
- ___
- ___
- ___
- ___
- ___

ROUTINES AND RITUALS

MORNING ROUTINE:

5am
6am
7am
8am
9am
10am
11am

AFTERNOON ROUTINE:

12pm
1pm
2pm
3pm
4pm
5pm
6pm

EVENING ROUTINE:

7pm
8pm
9pm
10pm
11pm
12am

TODAY'S BEST MOMENT:

DAILY ACHIEVEMENTS

WORK:

PERSONAL:

EXERCISE:

FOOD:

MINDSET:

FUN:

DAILY GRATITUDE:

WORK FROM HOME
daily planner

TOP 3 WORK PRIORITIES:
- ○ _____
- ○ _____
- ○ _____

TOP 3 PERSONAL PRIORITIES:
- ○ _____
- ○ _____
- ○ _____

WORK TO-DO LIST:
- ○ _____
- ○ _____
- ○ _____
- ○ _____
- ○ _____
- ○ _____
- ○ _____
- ○ _____
- ○ _____
- ○ _____

PERSONAL TO-DO LIST:
- ○ _____
- ○ _____
- ○ _____
- ○ _____
- ○ _____
- ○ _____
- ○ _____
- ○ _____
- ○ _____
- ○ _____

RESOURCES NEEDED TO SUCCEED:
- ○ _____
- ○ _____
- ○ _____
- ○ _____
- ○ _____

RESOURCES NEEDED TO SUCCEED:
- ○ _____
- ○ _____
- ○ _____
- ○ _____
- ○ _____

ROUTINES AND RITUALS

MORNING ROUTINE:

5am
6am
7am
8am
9am
10am
11am

AFTERNOON ROUTINE:

12pm
1pm
2pm
3pm
4pm
5pm
6pm

EVENING ROUTINE:

7pm
8pm
9pm
10pm
11pm
12am

TODAY'S BEST MOMENT:

DAILY ACHIEVEMENTS

WORK:

PERSONAL:

EXERCISE:

FOOD:

MINDSET:

FUN:

DAILY GRATITUDE:

> **There isn't a person anywhere who isn't capable**

of doing more
than he thinks
he can.

"

– HENRY FORD

MINDSET

I love starting the day with the right plan and mindset. It helps me anticipate issues and keeps me enthusiastic about the day ahead. The most common thing among successful people is that they have all established a solid morning routine that they stick to every day. Some wake up at the crack of dawn and go out exercising, while others sleep longer, meditate and make a big breakfast.

Whatever it is, knowing the way you want to start the day and actually committing to doing that every day will put you in the best mindset possible and set the tone for the rest of your day.

Finishing the day **appreciating the achievements** and the learnings will prepare your mindset for tomorrow. A little spot of **gratitude and reflection** never goes amiss.

So often we just keep on keeping on, day after day, without pausing to give ourselves a pat on the back for what we've accomplished that day and pause a moment to think about any challenges or what we need to get done tomorrow.

With good leadership and good personal initiative, there's no question we can walk the walk, **but how can we talk the talk, when the talk is coming at us all the time?**

Location freedom means a world of chat, emails, apps, group chats and a whole suite of written word dialogues. You would have particularly noticed this in the initial few days of switching from an office to working from home – almost all of them were spent setting up **WhatsApp** groups and asking "Can you hear me?" on video calls.

As you get used to not being able to just quickly shout a question to someone at the desk across from you, you'll have to get familiar with how to communicate with your team and strike a good balance with the amount of times you're messaging someone – no one wants that overbearing type popping into their notifications every five minutes.

The whole point of working from home means **less distractions**, and it's an amazing process to go through as you realise what communications are the important ones, and which ones were just chewing up your time when you were working in the office.

It also takes some time to learn how to communicate digitally when you're physically removed from others. Without faces or tone, it can be harder to discern what the other person is trying to tell you. The voice in their head that they've used to type the message is completely different from the voice in your head that you've used to read the message.

You need to learn to walk before you can run and we need to enter this stage with a beginner's mind.

WHY IS THIS IMPORTANT?

We've all had that texting drama where party number one fires off an innocent text to party number two and gets no response, and party number one is left wondering why they never got a response. Then they finally find out through party number three that something in party number one's text actually had offended party number two.

The written word without visual or verbal cues can be a recipe for miscommunication. When we're not in the same office building as someone else, **how can we make sure that we are communicating in the best way possible so our intent is received in the correct way?**

Simply put, we're not avatars in a computer game – we're humans. Just because we're going digital, doesn't mean we can forget the heartbeats. Nourish the humanity in your team in the everyday interactions that bond us and you'll create a buzzing office vibe even with your team all working in different locations from home.

TIPS FOR CLEAR COMMUNICATION

REMEMBER, YOU'RE NOT ABOUT TO BUMP INTO YOUR COLLEAGUE IN THE KITCHEN AND SMOOTH THINGS OVER WITH A CUPCAKE. HERE'S A FEW GROUND RULES TO AVOID CONFLICT AND FEELINGS GETTING HURT.

Context – Since we're all communicating digitally you can't tell what the person you're chatting to is feeling, so a one word response could seem cold, angry or even rude. Take a minute longer to construct a proper, clear and helpful reply.

Time – With so many great tools to convey information, having a few rules can be so helpful around timelines. Is the information needed fast? Jump on the phone for a quick chat. Is there more lead-time? Map it out on a project management app like Trello or Asana.

Content – Is the discussion around offering feedback? Virtual face-to-face is best. You both want to see body language and facial expressions when delivering and receiving difficult information.

@LISAMESSENGER

BE YOUR BEST. BE YOUR BEST. BE YOUR BEST. BE YOUR BEST. BE YOUR BEST. BE YOUR BEST. BE YOUR BEST. BE YOUR BEST. BE YOUR BEST. BE YOUR BEST.

BE YOUR BEST

some fun

Here's a good little exercise.

Read the following sentence out loud five times, putting emphasis on a different word each time.

'CALL ME A TAXI PLEASE.'

There are five completely different meanings in this one innocent phrase, depending on **which word you emphasise.**

In written form, we, the receiver of the communication, create meaning from our own internal voice – not the sender's.

Good communication isn't just what you say, but how you say it. Sometimes, even putting emphasis on the wrong syllable can end in tears. This is even more true for your client and customers, especially if they are used to doing business with you face to face.

You'll have to think carefully during this time about shifting your communication from in-person to digital for any external stakeholders.

For quick, efficient communications, words on a screen are fine. However, if your purpose is to **build relationships** and **ensure the meaning is conveyed and understood correctly**, then video or picking up the phone are much better mediums.

Body language and tone of voice are two components that make up a huge part of communication, so if you can utilise a tool that adds at least one of these to the words that are being said then that will help you communicate more effectively.

Not only that, making the time for a phone or video call will also show the person you're reaching out to **that you care,** which is another great bonus.

A human voice is worth a thousand words.

66

As far as this business of solitary confinement goes, the most IMPORTANT thing for survival is COMMUNICATION with someone, even if it's only a WAVE or a WINK, a tap on the wall, or to have a guy put his THUMB UP. It makes ALL the difference.

– JOHN MCCAIN

99

LET'S ALL CARE A LITTLE MORE ABOUT EACH OTHER.

6

PLAY

YOUR MINDSET IS THE FOUNDATION FOR CREATING ANYTHING – SO, LET'S GET YOU REALLY THINKING ABOUT HOW YOUR MINDSET IS NOW, AND HOW WE CAN IMPROVE IT!

Firstly, **how did you like filling out the Work From Home Planner?** I'd love to see how you used yours! Share some pics with me on Insta **@lisamessenger.**

Think about a time in your life where something pretty bad happened. Write about it here:

___
___
___
___

What did you do to overcome this situation? Did you use some methods of self-care? List them here:

___
___
___
___

When was there a moment when you felt an overwhelming feeling of joy? Write about it here:

_____
_____
_____
_____

What were the series of events that lead to you feeling this way?

_____
_____
_____
_____

Think about ways you can use these moments in future to create more joy. Write about it here:

_____
_____
_____
_____
_____
_____

What are you most grateful for right now? Why?
_____
_____
_____

Who are your support people? Why do you think they offer you so much? Why are you grateful for them?
_____
_____
_____

How can you be that person to other people? Do people rely on you for joy and energy? How can you be more like this to people in your network?
_____
_____
_____

How do you feel after answering these questions? Rate your mindset now, out of 10 and explain why:
_____
_____
_____

Notes/comments/takeaways/ideas:

> Challenges are what make life interesting.

Overcoming them
is what makes
life meaningful.

"

- JOSHUA MARINE

chapter seven

YOUR WORKFORCE

WORK IS WHERE THE HEART IS.

BY NOW, YOU HAVE YOUR WHY. YOU'VE GIVEN FEAR THE FLIP. YOU HAVE A PLAN TO NAIL YOUR LOGISTICS, AND THE TOOLS, TIPS AND TRICKS NEEDED TO EFFECTIVELY DECENTRALISE YOUR TEAM ARE READY TO BE PUT INTO ACTION.

You're leading with heart. Now that that's all down pat, it's time to focus on your number one asset – your workforce, or, if you fly solo, yourself.

Some companies take a 'move the lot' approach, and with COVID-19 that may have already happened, albeit on the fly. We're still in the design stage and that's exciting because the floodgates are flung wide open to opportunity.

Freelancers? The gig economy is growing and the progressive companies are searching for your expertise – you now have a world of job opportunities to tap into.

Entrepreneurs? There's an infinite raft of new platforms, prospects and ideas to pioneer.

The team leaders? Your human resources department just went global. No longer do your best recruits have to be living a home-run from your headquarters. You can now attract brilliant talent from anywhere in the world who can bring their skills to take your organisation to new heights. When you put up a job ad, the best brains in the business are now batting for you.

I have highly successful friends working for global icons whose headquarters are in Paris, Milan and Washington, and they each work from their own postcodes right here in Australia. **That is what we call location freedom.**

We are literally a workforce on the move. Solopreneurs can create a beautiful blend of work and life while exploring the far-reaching corners of the globe. Wi-Fi means that, as long as you have your laptop, you can **plug in anywhere** and get your work done.

Many managers are seeing the improvements in employee output when those team members have the freedom to travel and live where they like.

For now, we're all in this together. No one really knows what the future of work will look like, but I know that it will have more heart than before.

Now is the perfect time to create your best work/life routine! Don't miss this chance to implement all your most loved activities into your every day.

@LISAMESSENGER

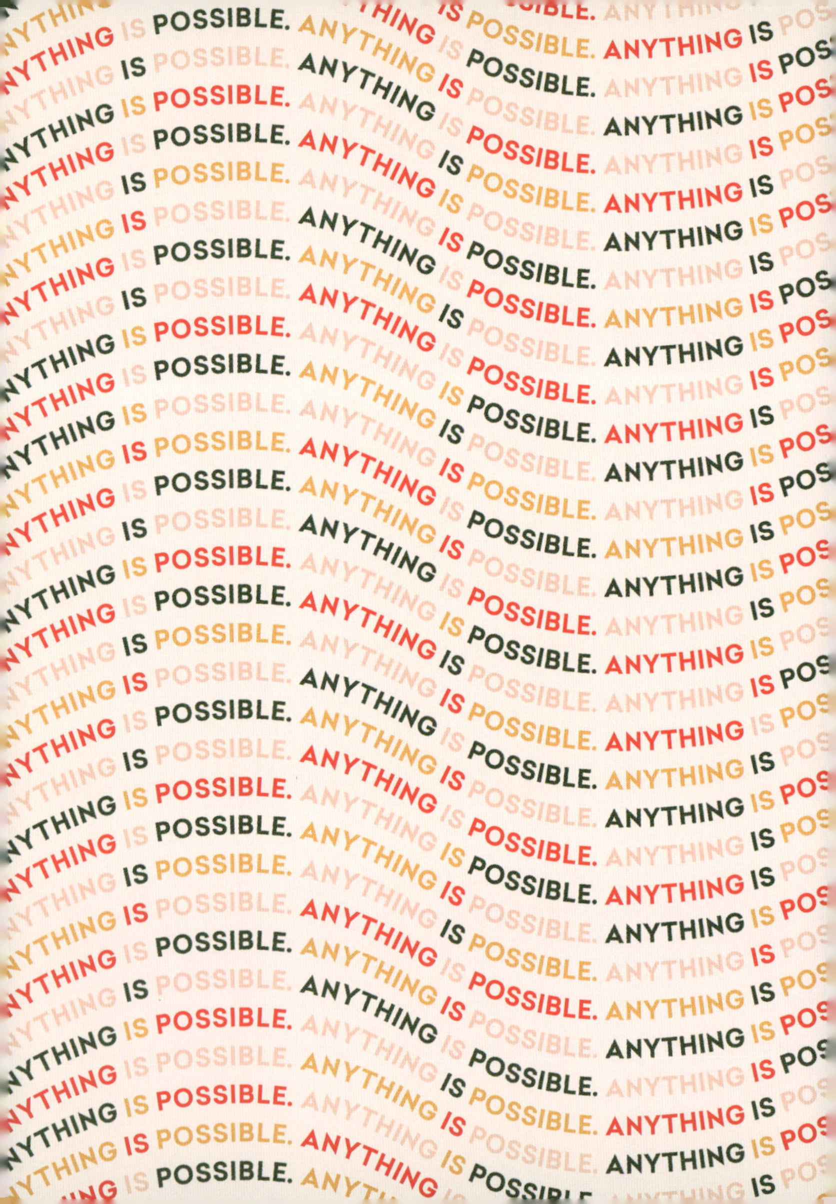
ANYTHING IS POSSIBLE.

During COVID-19 we saw millions laid off, yet innovative thinkers pivoted to create overnight labour exchange programs. We could see this option become part of the fully refurbished workforce, with transferable skills keeping companies in the black and workforces in work.

WHAT DOES THIS PROVE?
ANYTHING IS POSSIBLE!

We are the architects, redesigning from the ground up what was a pretty tired and weathered old model.

If we're honest, a lot of workers were exhausted and uninspired. They had lost sight of the 'why', merely going through the motions. Teams weren't working with heart, because they didn't have freedom in their lives. That's not a good combination for the **individual or the business**.

When *Collective Hub* had 34 full-time staff, only **three** were writers. Lightbulb moment!

Moving to a freelance model was great for the team, great for business and great for efficiency. When I needed a specialist in Berlin to write about technology, I had one. When I needed someone in New York to write about fashion, it was a done deal.

I could also make use of time zones around the world. While Australia slept, the United Kingdom was awake. That meant I could email an article brief at 7pm to a freelancer living in London and have it completed and returned by the time I woke up the next day. That is efficient.

I was already a decentralised founder before the pandemic. I had multiple channels, touchpoints and revenue streams, the most profitable of which were produced by **untethered talent** who were not on the payroll.

There are so many pluses for businesses and for workers who get to work in the comfort of their own homes, creating a life they love on their own terms.

The world is in a unique position right now. We have the chance to knock down the old house and rebuild a masterpiece. We can create the **future of work** that we always talked about and wished for and make it our **reality.**

So far, it has meant rolling up our sleeves, getting our hands dirty and turning up every day to face challenge after challenge, questioning how on Earth we're going to make this work.

Despite all the challenges, questions and the unknown, we're building something amazing.

We've seen the '#We'reAllInThisTogether' hashtag trending a lot during COVID-19 on our Instagram feeds, and it's this very attitude that not only pulls us all through the tough times, but sees us innovate and achieve some pretty amazing things.

It connects us all and brings us hope that we're forging this new path together.

HOW CAN WE PULL THIS ALL TOGETHER AND CREATE THE FUTURE OF WORK?

The answer is very simple – teamwork.

Even if you're a team of one, you are not alone. You can join networks, work with your existing ones and plug into a global team. We're going to connect, reach out, offer our services and knowledge, exchange ideas and come at it with a game plan, because **more minds are better than one.**

Do you manage a team? They'll jump on board too when they feel that they're part of this global rebuild.

I can't think of another event in our lifetime where the entire world was united. Think about the power and beauty of that!

No country pulling apart. **We are all one team.**

Do you remember during the peak of the outbreak? People were isolated in their own individual homes, but they were still united, and the world began to sing. Pub choirs became couch choirs. Balconies became stages for the isolated. People sang praise for the carers and medical staff as they passed by.

When we're united, we work.

That is exactly the magic we need right now to build this colossal new building – our ultimate **now of work.**

Thomas Edison wasn't the only one to come up with the idea of electricity. He was a collaborator, bringing together great minds who thought alike. Their collective light bulb moment (see what I did there) literally changed the world.

> *Where there is* UNITY *there is always* VICTORY.
>
> – PUBLILIUS SYRUS

> "Create the kind of workplace and company culture that will attract great talent. If you hire brilliant people, they will make work feel more like play."

– SIR RICHARD BRANSON

CASE STUDY
Airwallex

President and co-founder of Airwallex, Lucy Liu, shared some incredible learnings with me that really demonstrate team power.

Airwallex is an innovative global brand delivering cross-border payment technology that simplifies life for all of their clients. If you're doing business globally, I would highly recommend checking them out.

The Airwallex office in China was the first of the company's offices to be affected by COVID-19. Lucy and her co-founders strongly believed that social distancing was the best way to curb the spread, so they moved fast to implement work-from-home policies. They had no idea of the viral tsunami that was coming.

Locally in China, they experimented fast, and found **three key ways** that remote working worked, which they then rolled out to offices in Australia, the United Kingdom and the United States.

Let's dissect these.

1. First, they set out to simulate a virtual office environment.
Isolation – and the loss of the subsequent usual office chatter – could have had a profound impact on staff morale. They made it a priority that self-isolation would not be a lonely experience and set out to move opportunities for socialisation and catch-ups with coworkers online.

How did they do it?
They used the breadth of digital collaboration tools available to them so they could replicate a truly social experience. Slack and Zoom brought the team together in fun new ways. They created all-day Zoom rooms within team squads which allowed everyone to be connected. Anyone could pop-in and say hi or ask a question, just like they would be able to in the normal office building. Everyone had their Zoom cameras on for meetings so they could see each other's faces, introducing their pets to other pets and glimpsing each other's personal sides. That helped keep the same personal touch they were used to in the physical office building.

The Australian office came up with 'water and wine cooler' sessions for the whole team to come together at the end of each week and share stories of their work-from-home experiences – just like Friday afternoon drinks. Everyone brought their own drinks to their tables, and they each created custom backgrounds for some added entertainment and dazzle.

Keeping this sense of fun is so important because a workforce who play together, stay together, especially when everyone needs to hunker down and deliver that project, meet a deadline or ideate something amazing.

The play makes work flow.

2. The second part of the plan was to continue to foster a results-driven culture among their remote teams.
Fun was important but, just like any business, they had to also achieve results. With long-term remote working, Airwallex was initially concerned about productivity. Would they still get as much done?

To mitigate this risk, the leadership team continued to set daily and weekly goals for their teams. Each team member also created their individual daily plans and tracked progress against the most urgent priorities, increasing accountability with a deep focus on results.

Each team member was accountable for their performance, reporting weekly updates on progress to their managers. This might seem like a lot of reporting on their daily activities, but their China teams found these processes helped to drive focus, and the same feedback came from teams in Australia, the United Kingdom and the United States.

It's important to celebrate the progress we all make as a team. Even though we're not in the same physical space as our teammates, we are in the same corporate space, so make sure you share the wins as well as the work.

So, how does this relate to the solopreneur, entrepreneur or freelancer?
The deliverables are exactly the same. Tracking your own progress keeps you accountable so you can deliver the outcomes you want to the timelines promised. Then, make sure you celebrate your wins with bubbles over Zoom with a friend!

It's all about honouring commitments through accountability, so working remotely is not working invisibly.

There's nothing more soul-sucking than feeling like you're invisible.

As I'm sure many of you have experienced at least once in your life, you can feel surprisingly lonely in a physical workplace that's buzzing with activity. On the other hand, you can feel incredibly supported, inspired, valued and connected when you're sitting alone in your apartment immersed in a truly nurturing team culture. It's the how that's important.

3. The third key takeaway from Airwallex builds on what we've learned so far from other case studies about tailoring communication to customers and partners.

It's important to remember that it's not just the team who is transitioning to remote life. Customers too are having to give up face-to-face contact and could feel like just a number if it's not properly addressed.

Airwallex had to deal with widespread cancellation of events and meetings across the region, eliminating opportunities for face-to-face interactions. This could have been a potentially massive problem in terms of customer relationships. The same psychological challenges arise with client culture as with team culture.

How did they manage this?
Airwallex decided to reinvest resources into digital marketing and **WeChat** (a Chinese multi-purpose

messaging and social media mobile app) campaigns, creating groups for customers that they could broadcast content to, as well as communicating product updates and helpful information, all delivered with a personal touch. That's another important note – it's easy for us all to feel like just a number on digital platforms when there's no personal touch behind it.

For both your team and customers, what are the tools, platforms and resources you can use to bring people together under commonalities and create communications to make them feel valued?
What can you do for them that's different from what's been done before?

I love these takeaways from **Airwallex.** With their headquarters in China, they were at the forefront of the pandemic, pioneering a lot of the measures hundreds of companies took up globally as the virus spread. They learned what worked and what didn't, and were able to keep pivoting and reinventing as they rolled it out across other countries to streamline working from home for their global workforce.

How did they get there?
By using a little something called teamwork.

TEAM MAKES DREAM

WORK THE WORK.

Whether you're leading your team into the work-from-home environment, or you're an entrepreneur, solopreneur or freelancer, **everyone's better with a team**.

Teams look different for everyone – it might be a team of technology supporters, a team of creatives, a team of office assistants or a team of accountants. You can form a team of virtual help through technology tools and apps, as well as human networks who are out there connecting and sharing. We are all in construction, building our revolutionary new workforce from the ground up.

Everyone on the team brings different skills and ways of thinking to the table. Ensuring your team members have their say and contribute to the type of organisation that you want to be will take your team or organisation to the next level and help you all work better together.

So, here we all are on the world-wide job site. Companies that have built a culture of **playing hard and working smart** will attract the talent they want and the right kind of personalities to get things firing. You want creative, driven, aspirational, intrapreneurial, remote team players who are out-of-the-cubicle thinkers.

However, be mindful that it's a two way street – **what do these star players want and need from an employer?**

How are you going to create a team and organisation in which they can thrive and how can you set them up to do their best work?

A big paycheck talks, but it's not the deal-breaker. In fact, a recent Deloitte survey of 10,000 millennials across 36 countries and more than 1,800 Generation Z's in six countries revealed three perks that this generation of workers want.

They are:

1. FREEDOM
2. ETHICS
3. WORK-LIFE BALANCE

In emerging markets, the gig economy is attracting this world-changing talent pool in droves. This generation are choosing their work based on these integral values they hold, and the gig economy meets most of them – they have the freedom to choose their jobs and hours, and can therefore create a better work-life balance.

The flipside of this is micromanaging. Perhaps one of the most ineffective aspects of the old way, micromanaging exponentially decreases job satisfaction and shows employees the opposite of what we want to foster – distrust and disrespect.

> If your actions inspire others to dream more, learn more, do more and become more, you are a leader.

– JOHN QUINCY ADAMS

Anyone who has experienced micromanagement will know the stress that they experience as a result of having someone constantly breathing down their neck, criticising everything they do because it's not the way they would have done it and demanding things are done one way, and one way only. **Even writing this is panic-inducing!**

Old-school micromanagement doesn't have a place on this new frontier (the frontier being the home).

WHY IS HELICOPTER-PARENTING YOUR TEAM A REALLY BAD IDEA?

It freezes productivity – it's a morale zapper and breeds contempt. It slows workflow and results in burnout, and when that happens, they'll politely ask you to leave, or they will leave.

We're building the new way of work, and we have to leave the old methods that didn't serve us behind. Not only are we creating location freedom, but freedom in the entire way we work. This is a chance to not just shift work into our homes, but to shift the inefficient ways that we've been doing things to new methods of working.

We're all signing an unwritten contract to be accountable, take responsibility and honour our commitments.

The thing that micromanagers are missing is that the whole point of bringing people on to your team is so you have access to different skillsets and different thinkers.

Rigidly sticking to one way of doing things means that you're not bettering anyone's skills or abilities or growing as a team or organisation.

It's integral to lead by example, even if you're leading yourself. Create a culture and environment that's respectful and builds on everyone's brilliance – including yours.

Then you'll allow everyone's genius to bubble up and play.

> FLEXIBILITY *and*
> *diversity foster* LOYALTY.

@LISAMESSENGER

**WE'RE IN
THE MIDDLE
OF BUILDING
A NEW WAY
TO WORK.
IT'S TIME TO
REINVENT**

THE TRADITIONAL WORKING WHEEL AND PAY ATTENTION TO WHAT REALLY WORKS.

@LISAMESSENGER

7
PLAY

ARE YOU A TEAM PLAYER? DO YOU HAVE EMPATHY AND CREATE FREEDOM, TRUST AND GOOD RELATIONSHIPS WITH YOUR EMPLOYEES? LET'S FIND OUT! AND, LET'S WORK OUT SOME WAYS WE CAN ALL DO BETTER, TOO.

What are your best qualities as a team player/manager/boss or CEO?

_____
_____

What about your worst?

_____
_____

How can you turn these 'bad' qualities around to use them for good?

_____
_____

How are you coping working from wherever?

_____

What are you actively doing to help your team and colleagues through this new way of work?
_____
_____

What are some things you can improve on?
_____
_____

Who can help you improve these things?
_____
_____

Write down your thoughts about how you've been handling tricky to navigate situations or issues you've had to deal with over the past few months:
_____
_____
_____
_____
_____
_____

Are you keeping the team in-line and on-track with all their projects? How are you supporting them?

___

Write down all the amazing qualitites your team has and think about how much of an asset they are to you personally and toward the business:

___

Honestly, how well do you think your approach is received by your team members?

___

If your team could give you advice, what do you think they's say?

_____
_____
_____
_____
_____

If you think your team members would say something like this, it's more than likely they are thinking it. So, how can you take this advice constructively and use it to better yourself?

_____
_____
_____
_____
_____

Are you feeling more empowered? Are you feeling like you can be a better team player now?

_____
_____
_____

take note

It's so easy to get caught up in day-to-day life and just keep on going on doing the same old things, repeating the same old habits. These last few pages should have made you dive deep into your actions and how you treat people, especially those who you work closely with. It's time for actionable reflection. We all need improvment, so take your notes on board and implement the changes you need to be a better person, manager, boss and team player.

Now, reflect on your answers and write any thoughts/ideas/comments or opinions you may have. The aim is to completely fill these pages with how you've acted, how you will act moving forward and to strategise any changes you'd like to implement. Have fun!

_____
_____
_____
_____
_____
_____
_____
_____
_____
_____
_____
_____
_____
_____
_____
_____

BE CONCERNED. BE SINCERE. HAVE EMPATHY. PEOPLE NEED YOU AND YOU NEED PEOPLE.

NOW IS ABOUT LIFTING EACH OTHER UP AND OFFERING SUPPORT WHEREVER NEEDED.

@LISAMESSENGER

chapter eight

YOUR TOOLKIT

HOW ARE YOU FEELING? EMPOWERED TO DO YOUR BEST WORK AND BE YOUR BEST SELF? EXCITED FOR THE NOW? PLAYFUL? I SAID THIS EARLIER BUT IT'S WORTH REPEATING – THE PLAY MAKES WORK FLOW.

Now, we're going to dive into skilling and tooling up so we can master working from home. In this chapter I'll share with you the motherload of tricks that will give you complete remote control in setting up and streamlining your business while working from home.

Not only that, they will also enable you to take your business to new heights.

For the technophobes out there, it's time to flip fear again and get familiar with the amazing tools that technology has to offer us. There are apps and programs for every facet of business that we can login to at any time on our laptops or phones. This is how the magic happens.

We're talking hacks, gadgets, apps, office assistants, upskilling and systems that are cutting edge and will enable you and your team to do exceptional, highly-skilled work in the home environment.

We have literally seen the workforce of the future turbocharged to become the **now of work**. We need all the bells, whistles, pings, rings and dings to finetune this machine so it can run like a dream.

Leading up to the peak of COVID-19, physical events were either being cancelled or reimagined. As physical distancing became more widespread, the gig industry began to die.

It hit hard.

From this challenge, however, we saw some pretty punchy pivots begin to happen around the world. Global Citizen, who would normally have hosted their annual festival, created 'Together At Home', a global broadcast of live music from top musicians like Lady Gaga and Taylor Swift, all digitally streamed.

Massive conference events could also no longer play to thousands of people in a confined space. Hundreds of personnel couldn't bump-in PA systems, staging and production, let alone the thousands that were going to attend.

HOW COULD ANY OF THESE PHYSICAL EVENTS POSSIBLY GO AHEAD?

They too had to pivot.

Suddenly, small television studios were repurposed as sound stages that beamed keynote speakers into the living rooms of a mass digital audience. These studios were able to replicate a live stage environment, which was anything from quick messages for staff and stakeholders to full scale, all-day conferencing.

The uptake by audiences was, and still is, overwhelming.

Innovators led the charge on this, and it could just be that COVID-19 has given birth to a whole new conferencing experience added to the traditional, physical event arena.

The game has changed.

word of advice

It's important to approach these technological platforms with a beginners mindset, particularly if you're a bit technologically challenged (like me). We can often view technology as complicated and frustrating to navigate. It can be overwhelming, with so many different apps and websites, that we don't know what we should be using. In order to live in the now of work, we need to drop any of these pre-existing attitudes and view technology as the exciting universe it is that will allow us more ease and excellence in our everyday work and for our business.

@LISAMESSENGER

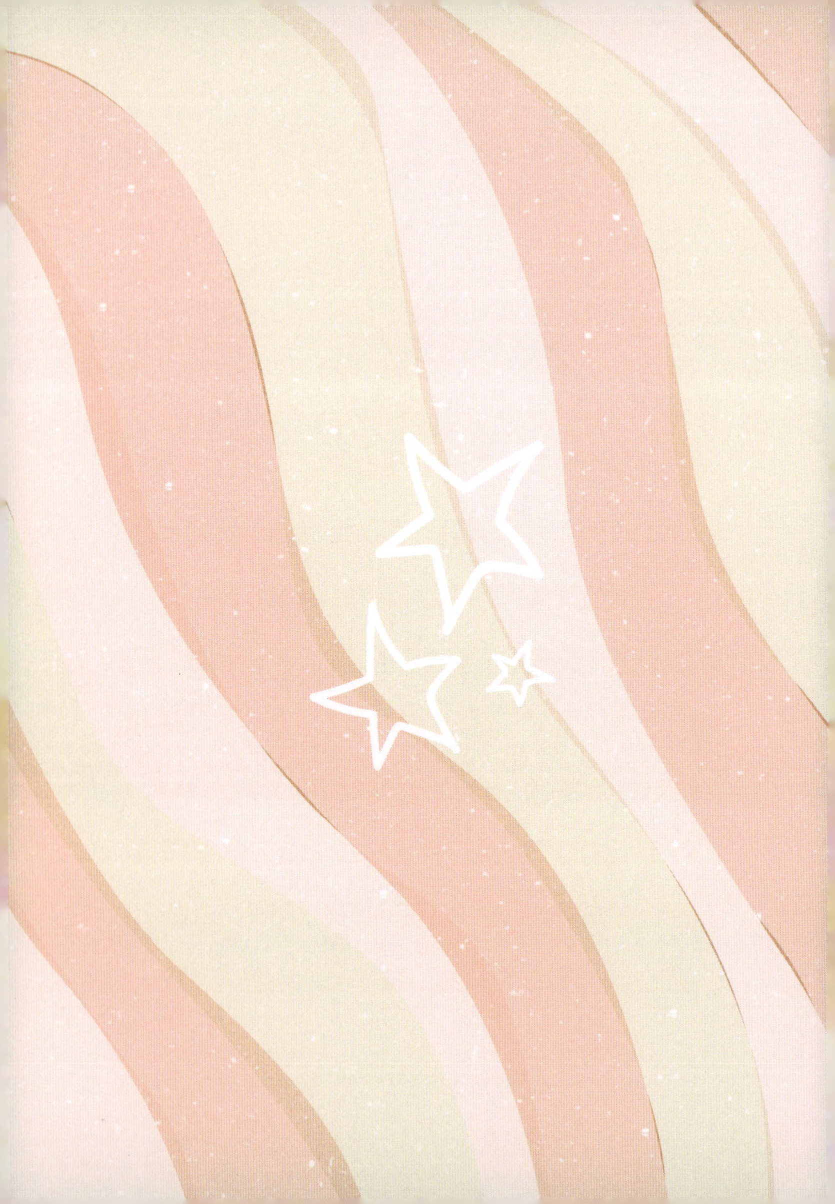

> **Let's go invent tomorrow instead of worrying about what happened yesterday.**

– STEVE JOBS

CASE STUDY
QODE Convention and Expo

This is the story of a pretty spectacular pivot.

The team behind QODE Convention and Expo, a massive technology convention that was just days out from their two-day live event involving thousands of ticket holders, exhibitors and speakers, was faced with cancellation.

Either the event had to be cancelled completely or moved online. The sheer logistics of making this happen in just two days would be enough to make anyone go into a meltdown. Since they were the 'techsperts', however, this was their game. They quickly got to work repurposing their convention.

The venue was transformed into a studio and event content was adjusted for the new online format. Speakers pivoted to address the COVID-19 crisis and the event futurist, Dr. Roey Tzezana, presented an entire address on the new theme – **the future of work.**

As the employment market was going through the largest scale shift in modern history at this moment, they completely nailed the messaging and content.

QODE became one of the first teams in the world to move an entire event (theirs being a conference and expo) into the virtual space, while still delivering the same value of a physical format and exhibitors.

Chief QODE Officer, Jackie Taranto, performed the ultimate pivot, using the situation to demonstrate innovation within an innovation-focused event.

This is a perfect example of what happens when ideas meet technology.

QODE was virtualised on the YouTube live platform, hitting 15,000 views in mere hours!

Necessity really is the mother of invention, and QODE pulled off a power pivot that likely pioneered this brave new conferencing play.

PIVOT

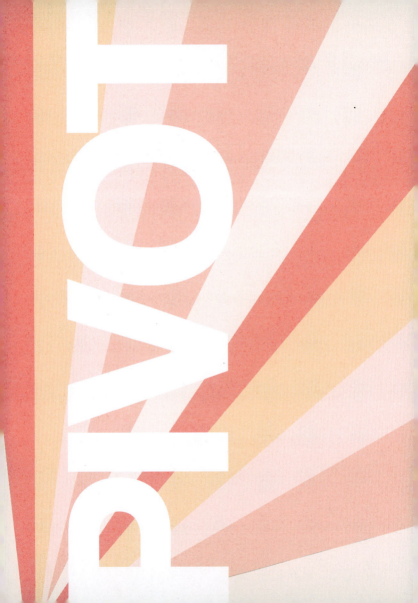

> **It is not the strongest or the most intelligent who will survive but those who can best manage change.**

– CHARLES DARWIN

CASE STUDY
Nova Entertainment

Another enormous pivot was demonstrated by Nova Entertainment, who moved their entire national broadcasting network to the bedrooms of their on-air announcers.

Transmitting FM bandwidth is a complex operation. Look behind your home television set-up – it's like spaghetti with all those wires and cables.

For a radio station, we're talking enough cables and hardware to take up a small house. Can you imagine that radio set-up in your living room?!

Nova Entertainment definitely had their work cut out for them.

What did they do?
Toolkits were dispatched to each announcer's home, along with a quickly compiled manual called *Remote Broadcasting for Dummies*.

What was unthinkable the week before became Nova's new now of work, rolled out in days with no dead air – they didn't miss a beat.

That's a supernova technical leap into the home.

You're not likely to launch an FM radio station in your pyjamas from your bedroom, but the example really drives home (pun intended) how technology can create almost magical wonders.

NOW, LET'S LOOK AT SOME CRAFTY TECHNOLOGICAL TOOLS WE CAN LOAD INTO YOUR KIT.

THERE ARE SO MANY OUT THERE, AND MORE ARE BEING DEVELOPED EVERY DAY. THE TOOLS BELOW ARE A GREAT PLACE TO START TO SET UP YOUR DIGITAL 'OFFICE' OPERATIONS. FROM THERE, IT'S REALLY A MATTER OF DRILLING DOWN ON WHAT YOUR SPECIFIC NEEDS ARE AND WHAT TOOLS WILL HELP YOU WORK BOTH SMART AND FAST.

TRELLO:

This is your new virtual office with at-a-glance status updates, meeting agendas and all things project management. If not being in the office is leaving you feeling frazzled when it comes to managing your team's workload and keeping up with all the different projects going on in your organisation, this one's for you. You can create a board (great for visual thinkers), a team or a business team, and it's in real-time so everyone can follow projects and timelines. It's for collaboration and project status. If you're visual like me, you'll love it for its colour-coded post-it notes.

ZOOM:

This is your go-to video conferencing tool and can handle anywhere from one to hundreds of participants. There's also a chat tool for commentary throughout the meeting, which is perfect if you have lots of people on the call. Early in the mass uptake during COVID-19, security did become a concern for a small period of time, but the company has since implemented extra layers of protection. You can use Zoom for your work meetings or to host live events, such as educational webinars. There's also in-built tools to record conversations – once you explore the functionality of this tool it will become your one-stop shop for all things communication.

CONFLUENCE:

This is a fantastic internal communications and collaborations tool. It helps teams share ideas, builds community, and is a great place to plonk your employee handbook or publish a blog. For anything company policy oriented, Confluence is your friend.

MICROSOFT TEAMS:
This is one of the better options for high-security needs because it's authenticated by the user. Conversations are private and secure, which is why Microsoft Teams was used at the highest levels during COVID-19 among first responders, governments, doctors and nurses in critical care units, researchers collaborating to develop a vaccine and teachers with children's privacy to protect. You can still do fun stuff too, but there's that extra layer of security, so you don't have Hamish Blake hijacking your boardroom meeting!

GOOGLE DOCUMENTS:
Personally, I love Google Documents. I collaborate with external partners and freelancers on hundreds of projects. Wherever we are in the world, we can all simultaneously edit, comment, and chat back and forth about particular sections of the document. Whether you're working on a long-form article in Word or compiling a list of clients in Excel, Google Documents has you covered.

SLACK:

I touched on Slack earlier and I love it because it replaces endless email threads – isn't that the dream! It's an instant messaging tool where you can chat to your team members and create a dedicated announcement channel and have all the info in one place. It also brings all of your most useful apps together like Outlook Calendar, Google Drive, Dropbox, Salesforce, Box (for file management)...the lot. Slack (as the name doesn't suggest) integrates with everything you're already using, so it helps you work more efficiently.

ASANA:

This is great for managing your projects. You can post status updates, tag coworkers in comments so you can give updates and chat about the project, and with the new work from home model, you can mark yourself as 'away' to alert your team that, although you're at home, you're not at work. Asana is great for mapping out all the steps that go into a large project that you're working on with others, as you can assign different tasks within the project to anyone on your team.

These are just a handful of the tools out there to help you get started and streamline your business and team. They act as virtual assistants, helping you organise work and get stuff done, time-saving tools for communicating and collaborating, and also for keeping the fun in work.

Since you're no longer wasting hours in peak-hour traffic, why not schedule 30 minutes of training into your day and wise up on all the tools that will help your team.

Register for a free webinar, listen to a podcast, sign up for any number of free virtual training programs offered by all of these apps and platforms and get the know-how on all the tricks of the work from home trade.

I know it might sound super overwhelming to the virtual office newbie, but once you define what you need as a solopreneur, entrepreneur or team player, then having the right tools will make everyone's jobs so much easier.

It's about working smart and utilising the tools that are available to help us do just that.

Digital Asset Management software (or DAMs) are the hacks that will bring everyone together and uplevel your work tasks.

Whatever the tasks or projects that you're working on are, and whatever work issue you need to solve, rest assured there's an app or an online tool for that – so it's time to get searching.

Since COVID-19, the technology revolution has seen a doubling of advancements across every area of the digital space.

There are now user-friendly programs and software for the tasks that used to take us hours and hours a couple of years ago. Technology is freeing up more time for us than ever before to focus on the things that actually require our human brains and presence.

If we make friends with it, we'll never feel alone, we'll never feel overwhelmed, and we'll be fully equipped to drive this **new workforce** into our completely re-designed future.

Change is growth, and growth is life.

We get to ride the wave with each new piece of information we tuck into our virtual backpacks. **Let's grow together!**

There's so much education out there and it's all at your fingertips.

some fun

Stop! Your exercise right now, in this very moment, is to jump on **TED Talks** and watch three talks of your choice. On the next few pages, list the **five best takeaways** from each and explain how you can implement them into your life.

@LISAMESSENGER

TED TALK NUMBER ONE:

TAKEAWAY ONE.
_____
_____
_____

TAKEAWAY TWO.
_____
_____
_____

TAKEAWAY THREE:
_____
_____
_____

TAKEAWAY FOUR.
_____
_____
_____

TAKEAWAY FIVE.
_____
_____
_____

chapter eight: your toolkit

TED TALK NUMBER TWO:

TAKEAWAY ONE.
_____
_____
_____

TAKEAWAY TWO.
_____
_____
_____

TAKEAWAY THREE:
_____
_____
_____

TAKEAWAY FOUR.
_____
_____
_____

TAKEAWAY FIVE.
_____
_____
_____

TED TALK NUMBER THREE:

TAKEAWAY ONE.
_____
_____
_____

TAKEAWAY TWO.
_____
_____
_____

TAKEAWAY THREE:
_____
_____
_____

TAKEAWAY FOUR.
_____
_____
_____

TAKEAWAY FIVE.
_____
_____
_____

EXPAND YOUR MIND. ENGAGE WITH NEW THINGS. TAKE NEW OPPORTUNITIES. TRAVEL.

EXPLORE. LISTEN. BE SWITCHED ON. YOU CAN LEARN SOMETHING FROM EVERYONE.

@COLLECTIVEHUB

8
PLAY

WE'VE SPENT THE LAST CHAPTER TACKLING YOUR TOOLKIT. YOU SHOULD BE FEELING PRETTY EQUIPPED BY NOW! GET READY, THIS SECTION IS BIG!

How are you feeling? Are you feeling motivated? Inspired? Or a little overwhelmed?
Use this page to put your thoughts to paper:

_____
_____
_____
_____
_____
_____
_____
_____
_____
_____
_____
_____
_____
_____

List out some strategies to make your tech-load a little more achievable and approachable:

_____
_____
_____
_____
_____
_____
_____
_____

List the tools that you've tried, tested and loved. How can you help implement these more efficiently across your workplace?

_____
_____
_____
_____
_____
_____
_____
_____

NOW IT'S TIME TO LEVEL UP YOUR ENERGY AND GET A HEALTHY DOSE OF INSPIRATION.

Go for a walk and listen to a new podcast. It can be about anything – something to escape your normal, or something to inspire!

What podcast did you listen to?

_____

Why did you like it? What did you learn?

_____

_____

Pick a night this week to be 'doco night' and sit back, relax and learn about anything your heart desires!

What doco did you watch?

_____

What did you learn?

_____

_____

List five of the most inspiring people you follow on Instagram.

1. _____

What are they an expert at?
_____
_____

Why do you follow them?
_____
_____

What can you learn from them?
_____
_____

If you were to meet this person, what would you ask them for advice on?
_____
_____

Now... direct message them and ask the question!!
You never know – they might reply!

2. _____

What are they an expert at?
_____
_____

Why do you follow them?
_____
_____

What can you learn from them?
_____
_____

If you were to meet this person, what would you ask them for advice on?
_____
_____

Yep, you have to ask the question to this one too :)

3._____

What are they an expert at?
_____
_____

Why do you follow them?
_____
_____

What can you learn from them?
_____
_____

If you were to meet this person, what would you ask them for advice on?
_____
_____

You guessed it, slide into their DMs and take a moment of courage to ask them your question – you never know!

4._____

What are they an expert at?
_____
_____

Why do you follow them?
_____
_____

What can you learn from them?
_____
_____

If you were to meet this person, what would you ask them for advice on?
_____
_____

And again...ask, ask, ask, you can do it! It should be getting easy by now!

5. _____

What are they an expert at?
_____
_____

Why do you follow them?
_____
_____

What can you learn from them?
_____
_____

If you were to meet this person, what would you ask them for advice on?
_____
_____

Lucky last – ask away. You've got this!

If you follow me, you'd already know that I'm a big believer in journaling. I love it! It provides a space for me to empty my ever revolving creative brain. Sometimes I need to get an idea on to paper, sometimes it's just musings from my day, and other times I need to have a rant! I'm only human. Over the next few pages, I want you to just write. Anything!

This is a great exercise to begin to understand some of the things your body and mind is craving or seeks.

Let's delve in, no rules, no inhibitions, just go:

_____
_____
_____
_____
_____
_____
_____
_____
_____
_____
_____
_____

Notes/comments/takeaways/ideas:

> In a time of drastic change it is the learners who inherit the future. The learned usually find themselves equipped to live in a world that no longer exists.

— ERIC HOFFER

chapter nine

DISCIPLINE
RITUALS
ROUTINES
BOUNDARIES

YOU ARE ACQUIRING SKILLS AND FEEDING A HUNGER THAT WILL FORM NEW HABITS FOR EITHER YOURSELF AND YOUR OWN BUSINESS, OR YOUR WORKFORCE.

These habits will keep you young, energised, plugged-in and valuable. **You have the knowledge and you have the goals.** Now, it's time to equip you with the processes that will help you achieve every goal you set yourself and help you work with purpose each and every day.

I want to touch on holidays for a moment.

I love holidays so much I made my work one long, work-from-wherever holiday! We all love the things that holidays bring us – a change of scenery, freedom, waking to no alarm, relaxing our diet rules, taking a break from the gym and indulging in some delicious cocktails (in my case, mocktails!) by the pool.

Holidays are a permission slip to take a break from our lives.

Yet, towards the end, part of you looks forward to getting back to routine. We notice a few extra kilos, the abs are no longer looking that fab, and you look forward to getting back into some work and a structured daily routine.

Working is good. **The freedom of working from home is awesome.** We just need to establish a system of discipline, rituals, routines and boundaries that keep us sharp, on-track and healthy.

Trust me, from years of experience, working from home requires more discipline than working at an office.

If future travel while working on-the-go is something you're working towards, then having structure in your day will give you a never-ending working holiday – and, as previously established, we all love holidays.

You'll be able to merge adventure, ambition, exploration, success and new experiences, all the while living your purpose.

A work-life blend is the magic you can look forward to.

There's no more wishing you could escape the office or waiting all year for those few weeks off where you can enjoy your freedom. What used to be your 'work' and your 'life outside work' are now rolled into one.

I've been doing it for years and I'm living my best life.

I want you to look forward to living your best life too, wherever we eventually all land.

> *Happiness is an ATTITUDE. We either make ourselves miserable, or happy and strong. The amount of work is the SAME.*
>
> – CARLOS CASTANEDA

CREATE DISCIPLINE.

PRACTISE YOUR RITUALS.

STICK TO YOUR ROUTINE.

ESTABLISH BOUNDARIES.

@LISAMESSENGER

my routine

My routines change as the seasons do, so right now this is how my day looks:

7.30AM

I wake up and start the day with yoga on my deck for an hour, finishing with ten minutes of savasana meditation. This practice really sets me up for the day ahead.

8.30AM

I make a green smoothie and jot down a few things I'm grateful for that day to help me smile as I head into the day. Podcasts, writing and self-education happens from then until about 10am, so by this stage I've filled my mind with good things and kept my body strong in a proactive way.

10AM

It's game on from here.
I'm in reactive and responsive
mode as I start my work day.

6PM ONWARDS

I'll either stop working
or do some more work
if needed or I feel like it.

Otherwise, it's time
to wind-down.

word of advice

This is what works for me, but it will look different for everyone. You might still be required to work the same or similar hours as you did at the office, but now you can use the time you would normally spend commuting to get into some routines and rituals that help you start and end the day in a way that works for you. If you're a solopreneur or flexible with when you work, it's a good time to re-examine your routine and make sure that it's working for you.

Now is the perfect time to start testing how you would like to schedule your day to set yourself up in the best possible way.

In this chapter, we're going to create **disciplines, rituals, routines and boundarie**s that work for you, and then also address creating these for the wider team (if you have one).

Health is priority.

This includes your emotional health, social health, physical health and spiritual health – we need to be healthy in all areas of our lives. If we didn't have our health, we wouldn't be able to do the amazing things that we do every day.

For our minds to function as optimally as possible, we need to dedicate the time and the space to looking after ourselves properly.

Solopreneurs, entrepreneurs and freelancers, you are free to work your clock, your way. That might mean setting the alarm for 6.30am to meditate, go for a dawn run or listen to a podcast while making a healthy breakfast, then starting work a little earlier.

For others, you might like to sleep later, do your routines and work later in the day.

Whatever works for you, mindset and mindfulness from the moment you wake are the keys to work-from-home success.

As we touched on earlier, once you nail that morning routine you're setting yourself up for a **successful day.** You also want to make sure that you're eating nourishing foods throughout the day, moving your body and also **prioritising time in your week to rest.**

It's a big jigsaw puzzle with lots of different elements that all need to come together to make a healthy whole. It's time to make wellness your priority.

Remember, we're reinventing the workforce, **which means also reinventing you.** The old ways included sacrificing our physical, mental, spiritual and emotional health all for the rat race. We've known that that doesn't work and isn't sustainable for a while now, yet still ignored it. Now is the time that changes. Don't bring home what wasn't working in the office before.

some fun

Write out a wellness routine that you can incorporate into your work day. Dedicate time for each aspect in ways that work for you. If you're on the company clock, you likely can't put your out of office on and hit the beach at 3pm, so remember to be practical and design a day that you can achieve and also fits the rules.

5AM:

6AM:

7AM:

8AM:

9AM:

10AM:

11AM:

12PM:

1PM:

2PM:

3PM:

4PM:

5PM:

6PM:

7PM:

8PM:

9PM:

10PM:

11PM

THERE ARE SO MANY SIMPLE AND WONDERFUL WAYS TO TEND TO YOUR WELLBEING. LET'S BREAK DOWN THOSE DIFFERENT AREAS.

PHYSICAL WELLBEING

When we mention health, our physical wellbeing is often the first thing that our minds jump to, as it's the one that we're taught the most about growing up.

Eating nutritious and good-quality food is a must for our everyday functioning. Finding a way of fitting exercise in every day is also so important not only for our bodies but our mind. My brain feels so much clearer and ready to get stuck into work after I've done my morning yoga or clocked in some time on my treadmill.

MENTAL AND EMOTIONAL WELLBEING

Looking after our mental health should be at the top of our priority list, especially when you work from home.

We don't want stress to start seeping into our homes and taking over. Make sure you're taking proper breaks throughout the day and not over-working.

Getting into the habit of doing a regular mindfulness or meditation practice will help you clear your mind and remain calmer throughout the day, and using those project management apps will help keep you scheduled and focused.

Booking in moments for connection at the start of your week is also a great thing to do for your emotional wellbeing – these might be coffee dates, hikes, or phone calls and FaceTime catch-ups.

SPIRITUAL WELLBEING

This is one of the areas of our wellbeing that is often overlooked, as some people think it relates to religion or is only for 'woo woo' people.

However, our spiritual wellbeing relates to ourselves, our purpose and connecting with the world around us.

I look after my spiritual wellbeing when I take a walk out in nature. I also look after my spiritual wellbeing when I take time to check-in with myself, do fun activities that I enjoy and am working in alignment with my purpose.

You can see how these areas all overlap, and how just one activity can tend to multiple facets.

For example, going for a walk on the beach is great for my physical, mental and spiritual wellbeing.

It can be overwhelming looking at all the parts of yourself that we have to look after, so my advice is to start small and gradually build upon your habits, and to remember that you don't have to do everything.

Your life also doesn't have to look like the life of that health guru you follow on Instagram – just do what feels right for you.

FOR THE TEAM

Nova Entertainment is a fantastic example because it's a technology company in the media business, but built on fun.

Don't get me wrong, Nova Entertainment is a serious, revenue generating business requiring year-on-year growth and delivering commercial results for clients and stakeholders in a vastly changing media environment. Internally, however, the talent in all departments comes from creative, innovative, free-thinking individuals who each bring their unique sparkle to the table.

WHAT DISCIPLINES, RITUALS, ROUTINES AND BOUNDARIES DID THEY CREATE TO KEEP THE CULTURE BUZZING AND THE REVENUE FLOWING?

Weekly staff meetings where they all sat on bean bags were always a noisy and boisterous celebration in the office of the week's achievements. These included mandatory fun and games and a whip around from the leadership team who communicated upcoming on-air events and sales activity.

These staff meetings are a ritual that bonds the team. The executives knew that a boring email summary could not replace this opportunity for connection.

From home, these important staff meetings continued using **Microsoft Teams**, and they made it a dress-up theme. Every staff member was put in their own 'house', just like at school, and points were awarded for various activities, including Best Dressed.

To keep the bond, Nova even came up with the 'Bonds Award' – an enormous pair of Bridget Jones' style Bonds underwear gifted to the winner!

To keep Nova Entertainment running business as usual, all of their rituals and routines pre-COVID-19 needed to continue as stations around the network were hurriedly decentralising.

Budgets, reporting, KPIs, accountability, planning sessions, efficiencies and fun all migrated to their new, broadcasting-from-home operations.

You can see how structure – from setting up solid disciplines, routines, rituals and boundaries – is **absolutely essential** for work culture and wellbeing, whether working solo or with a team.

some great ideas

Help your team set boundaries at home.
Encourage them to communicate to anyone else at home that this is work time to maintain structure and clear boundaries. This also means reminding staff to take regular breaks and prioritise their physical and mental health.

Start the workday with a daily huddle.
This will reaffirm your team's cohesion. Encourage regular check-ins throughout the day or messaging within the team on platforms like Slack.

Streamline emails.
We don't want to bog each other down by emailing every small little thing to each other and filling up everyone's inboxes. Talk your team through a few email tricks to practise, such as: clear subject lines, no 'Reply Alls' unless necessary and bolding important points and due dates.

Schedule wellbeing practices.
Some teams like to do the 3pm stretch, or you might like to pop in 10 minutes of midday mindfulness. Not only does a small break like this help everyone feel better and more productive, it will bring that element of play into the day.

Walk your walk.
Part of being a leader is also being a role model. If you're always frazzled and sending emails at all hours of the night, your employees will start to think that it's also expected of them to work late. Make sure that you're adhering to your work hours, taking performance breaks and logging off at an appropriate time to set a positive example.

Be available.
I'm often asked how I stay connected to my team when they're spread across the world. The question I ask in response is, "How connected do you feel to a complete stranger on Instagram simply by watching their daily Stories?" and I see a lightbulb turn on. Be relatable, be there to support them, and show that you're also a human just the same as they are.

Disciplines, rituals, routines and boundaries will look different for everyone and every organisation. There are so many resources and tools to help get yours in place.

For me personally, I love Asana because it really makes everyone feel plugged-in. The other plus is visibility. With everyone at home, managers can feel out of the loop on where a project is at. The flipside of that is team members can feel their managers can't see all the work they're producing.

With a tool like Asana, everybody sees, everyone is accountable and we all know who's working on what, wherever we all happen to be working from.

As I've touched on earlier, there are literally hundreds of tools in the digital shed, and they're all pretty sharp.

Find the tools that work for you, then use them to help you set up your disciplines, rituals, routines and boundaries.

APPS FOR WORK/LIFE BALANCE

Pause – simply set a time, smack in some earbuds and do what you're told by this audiovisual app to bring mindfulness to your day. I love starting the day with some mindfulness as it helps keep me stay present throughout the day.

Antisocial – Did you know that on average people touch their smartphones 2,617 times a day? This app tracks exactly how much time you spend on your device so you can be more mindful about your usage or use the app to block time-sucking social media and apps.

Silo – Selectively mute distractions, notifications and alerts on your phone. You can customise all the settings so you still won't miss important work calls but will control the visual pings that creep into your attention every 10 minutes.

Focus Booster – Harnessing the power of the Pomodoro Technique – an approach designed to increase productivity by tackling tasks in short bursts with breaks in between – this app combats the cycle of distractions by timing your work sessions and automatically creating a timesheet – which is perfect for you freelancers out there. If you're dropping the concept of working rigid hours and instead evaluating performance based on KPIs and output, this one's a goodie to have up your sleeve.

Let's assume we all have the work ethic needed to drive success of our own enterprise or that of the company's – if you didn't, you wouldn't be reading this book.

The rest is having the right equipment, including setting up your **disciplines, rituals, routines and boundaries, structures, systems, support, technological tools, skills, knowledge, networks, mentors, mindset and play** (because play makes light work of hard work). We've unpacked so many fun and creative ideas to keep things light.

My friend Adam Jacobs, the founder of Hatch (and formerly the founder of The Iconic) told me about the mindfulness mornings via video call that his team have started doing.

He explained that these really help to set the intention for everyone's day. They also do work from home bingo, and they have a Slack channel dedicated to sharing fun memes and posts to keep the play throughout the day.

From playlists to themed dress-ups, find ways that make the now of work the happy of work, and this will help you get through the toughest days.

I feel so incredibly blessed at *Collective Hub*. We are literally a hub of sharing and caring.

We're like JFK International Airport, with a thousand flights of knowledge coming in from hundreds of destinations, landing and unpacking valuable insights that get shipped off to anyone who needs them. **That is connection.**

Of course, some days I feel down like everybody else, and that's just a part of life. Not every day is going to look like your dream life and sometimes we get in funks or just have an off day, and that's totally normal.

The shut-down at the beginning of COVID-19 was completely overwhelming. However, then a gift would arrive in my inbox by way of an inspiring story, idea or pivot, and I was back to feeling energised and raring to help.

During challenging times, we all need to continue to help each other. **Reach out for help and be of service.**

Helping can be sharing a success story, like my amazing friend Paul Schulte who runs Prince of York Wine Bar and Restaurant in Sydney. **The crisis was unfolding.** I'd just lost a big gig and I was feeling pretty down about it. Then Paul's email came in, sharing how energised he was and that he was pivoting and still delivering quality food, drinks and music, bringing the Prince of York experience to his patrons and retaining 30% of revenue in a market that had shut down.

His email fired me up. We all need that sometimes, just as we then need to be the person to fire someone else up when they're in a funk.

Paul said he felt like a little speed boat. When everyone else was sinking, he was zipping over the waves turning one business into three and stopping along the way to offer help and support to people who needed it.

What a mindset, and what a learning.

Of course, not every business is pivotable. The losses are real, and there are no magic words to fix it all. Circumstances definitely play their part, **but the real secret is that mindset does the rest.** Paul was in the same situation as everyone else in the hospitality industry, but he pivoted like lightning and thought of an outside-the-box way that he could continue delivering to and serving his customers.

The best way to stay in a positive mindset is to share and care.

Enable a culture of sharing instead of hoarding and everybody wins. Sometimes all someone needs to get out of a funk or a bad day is a helping hand or a conversation with someone else who gets what they're feeling.

> **Once your mindset changes, everything on the outside will change along with it.**

— STEVE MARABOLI

Who would have thought that this crisis would reduce us to the Great Toilet Paper Debacle of 2020 – first-world problems!

Stripping shelves in a mad panic because somehow we thought we would not have enough toilet paper to survive was not only dumb, but disappointing for all of us who believe in the good of humanity. Not to mention, there was enough toilet paper for everyone if people weren't hoarding it.

In the business community, there's enough business to share ideas and not hoard them. We're **stronger, better and smarter** when we share our ideas, so be generous with them. I've seen this coming together everywhere, in every sector of our global community, just as you have too – applauding, cheering, singing, and all the creativity that circled social media with hilarious isolation videos and memes.

There were people reaching out to one another for video calls to maintain connection, and others sharing their best isolation tips online.

We really are all in this together. It's a powerful, seismic shift of humanity. We are all a part of it as we masterbuild our future.

There has been so much loss. People have lost their incomes, their businesses, their livelihoods and their lifelong savings. There has been an unspeakable loss of life, especially of our overseas neighbours.

This heartbreak will live with us forever.

The world has changed. It was also pretty sick well before COVID-19. So many workers were overworked and uninspired, stuck on the hamster wheel, feeling exhausted and disconnected.

Congested cities made crawling to work a miserable ride.

We were sacrificing the beautiful parts of our lives, like family, friends and travel, so we could spend our days in an office.

This created an economy of convenience and fast fixes. Our planet was crying out for us to just stop, and COVID-19 made us do just that.

Post-COVID-19, out of such unthinkable loss, we have the **now of work** and a new way forward. From here on in, **we will only gain.**

WE ARE
ALL IN

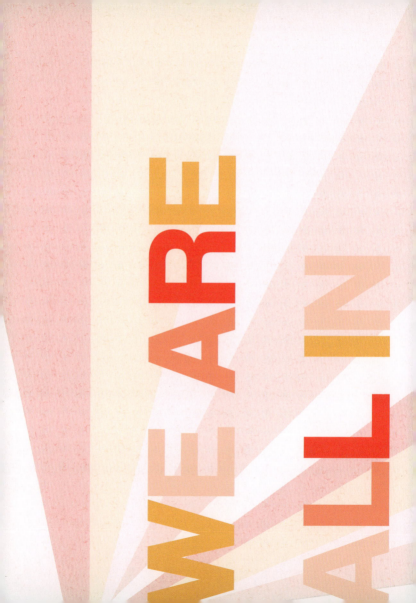

THIS
TOGETHER

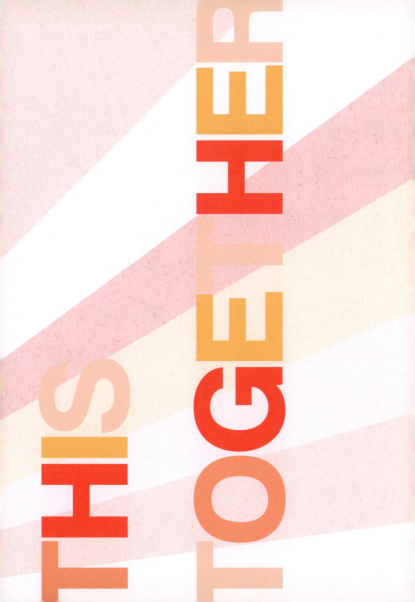

If you were dissatisfied with your life, perhaps working for someone else in a job that didn't fire you up and living life according to the expectations of others, now you have time and space to re-examine your purpose and how you want to be living your life.

So many of us for so long have said that we don't have that, but now COVID-19 has given us all the space and time to dig deep – it's a global reset.

We are ready to build something new, something different from what wasn't working for us before.

It's time to challenge old paradigms, go against the status quo, question our purpose and begin building the new future. We are living through history and we are the change.

This gives me goosebumps.

I'm so excited to be on this global job site and be part of the now of work with all of you.

Let's build this together!

> "There's a huge question mark on everything. It's a beautiful opportunity to change things, look at things differently and to evolve in a positive way."

— SILVIA VENTURINI FENDI

> **Do not sit still; start moving now. In the beginning, you may not go in the direction you want,**

> **but as long as you are moving, you are creating alternatives and possibilities.**

— RODOLFO COSTA

9
PLAY

YOUR HEALTH AND WELLNESS IS SO MUCH MORE IMPORTANT THAN THE TEST, THE GROCERY RUN, THAT UNREALISTIC DEADLINE, THE INTERVIEW... YOU OWE IT TO YOURSELF, TO PUT YOURSELF FIRST.

How's your mental and physical health? No matter who you are, I can garantee there's some part of your health that you can improve! Let's work out what you can do to be the best version of you.

Rate each out of 10:

Emotional health:

Social health:

Physical health:

Spiritual health:

Where is your biggest room for improvement?

_____
_____

What are some ways you can improve your scores?
___
___
___
___
___

How will you keep yourself on track?
___
___
___
___
___

Do you have any habits that will sabotage you? List them here:
___
___
___
___
___
___

List some things that make your heart sing:

_____
_____
_____
_____
_____

How can you include more of these things into your everyday life?

_____
_____
_____
_____

Sometimes we have to make sacrifices. What is something you like doing, but your time or energy could be better used toward your health?

_____
_____
_____
_____
_____
_____

Now let's jump into the nitty-gritty on disciplines, rituals, routines and boundaries (DRRBs). Write out what you currently do for each of these:

Disciplines:

Rituals:

Routines:

Boundaries:

How can your DRRBs improve? What areas are lacking? And why?

_____
_____
_____
_____
_____
_____
_____
_____
_____

When are you most productive in your day?
When are you most likely to have a crash?
Make some rules around when you will schedule in your most important tasks for your productivity window, and allow some time for rest and recovery during your low energy window. Listen to your body and hear what it needs. Write out your rules here:

_____
_____
_____
_____
_____
_____
_____
_____
_____
_____
_____
_____
_____
_____
_____

What are some challenges you could face?
___
___
___

Write a strategy for how you will deal with these challenges.
___
___
___

Go back to pages 192-201 and review your working planner. How was your output while keeping on track with the help of these planners?
___
___
___

What things could you include to help you on your personal journey?
___
___
___

Finally, write your purpose loud and proud using this space! Go big, go bold, and if you ever feel swayed, some back here and remember why you've written what you have.

MY PURPOSE:

Notes/comments/takeaways/ideas:

And just like that, you're done. I hope you feel excited and inspired for what's to come. All the best for your journey forward. I know with every cell of my body, that you're going to absolutely smash it!

Remember to share your journey with me @lisamessenger I absolutely love to see what you guys are up to, and would love to see how you've implemented your learnings from *The Now of Work*!

FIN.

About Lisa Messenger

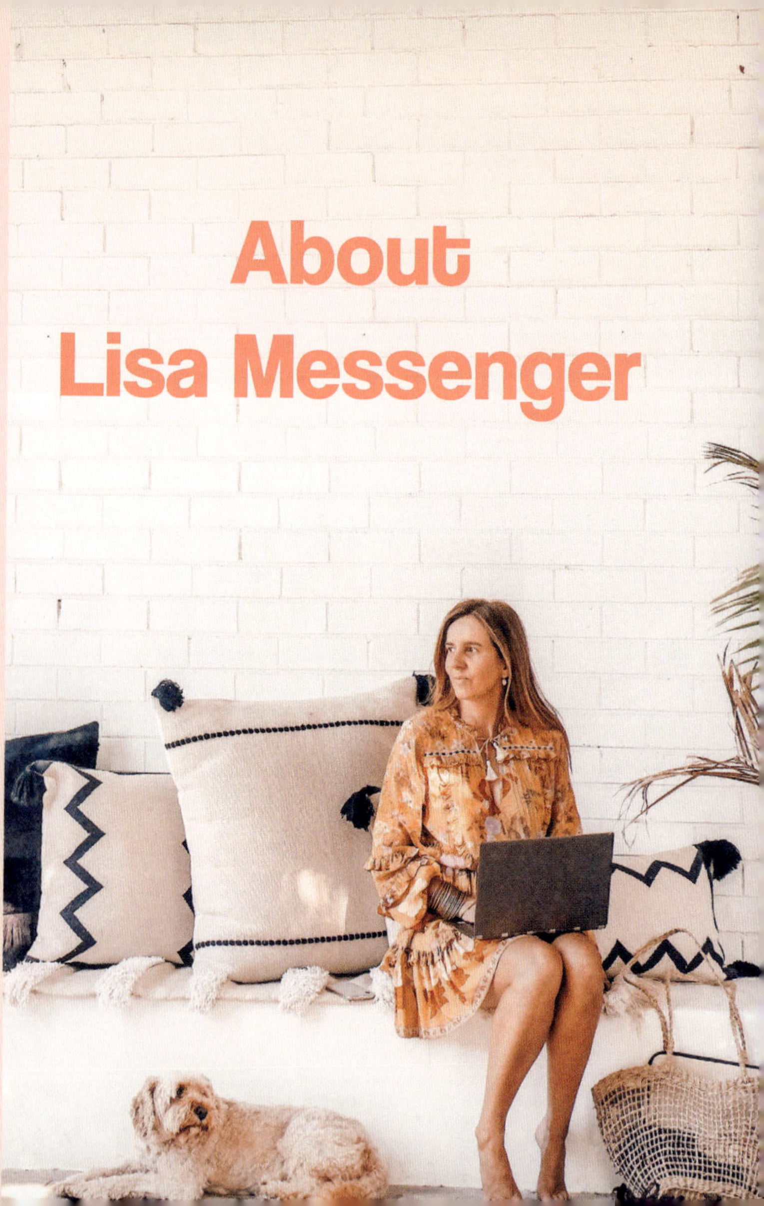

Lisa Messenger is the vibrant, game-changing founder and CEO of *Collective Hub*.

She launched *Collective Hub* as a print magazine in 2013 with no experience, in an industry that people said was either dead or dying. Over the next seven years, *Collective Hub* grew into an international multimedia business and lifestyle platform with multiple verticals across print, digital, events and a co-working space – all of which served to ignite human potential.

For more than 19 years in her own businesses, Lisa has inspired game-changers, thought-leaders, style-makers, entrepreneurs and intrapreneurs across the world.

An international speaker and best-selling author, she is an authority on disruption in both the corporate sector and the start-up scene. Lisa's experience in publishing has seen her produce over 400 custom-published books for companies and individuals as well as having authored and co-authored 27 herself.

Most notably, Lisa chartered her ride to success post-launch of *Collective Hub,* documenting the journey and all its lessons in real time with her best-selling book *Daring & Disruptive: Unleashing the Entrepreneur* and its sequels, which include *Life & Love: Creating the Dream; Money & Mindfulness: Living in Abundance; Break-ups & Breakthroughs: Turning an Ending Into a New*

Beginning; Purpose: Find Your Why and the How Will Look After Itself; Risk & Resilience, Breaking and Remaking a Brand; Work From Wherever: How to set yourself free and still achieve; and Daily Mantras To Ignite Your Potential.

Her passion is to challenge individuals and corporations to get out of their comfort zones, find their purpose, change the way they think, and to prove there is more than one way to do anything. She encourages creativity, innovation, an entrepreneurial spirit and lives life to the absolute max.

Most mornings she wakes up and pinches herself at how incredible her life is, but is also acutely aware and honest about life's bumps and tumbles along the way.

With fans including Sir Richard Branson and *New York Times* best-selling author Bradley Trevor Greive, and a social media following of more than 800,000 across her *Collective Hub* and personal platforms, Lisa's vision is to build a community of like-minded people who want to change the world.

In between being a serial entrepreneur, investor and avid traveller, she loves nothing more than being at home with her dog, Benny, doing some gardening and collecting as many indoor plants as humanly possible.

@lisamessenger #lisamessenger
@collectivehub #collectivehub

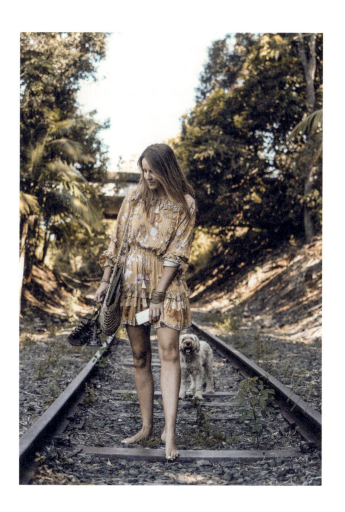

OTHER BOOKS BY LISA

WORK FROM
Wherever
How to set yourself free (and still achieve)
LISA MESSENGER
FOUNDER AND EDITOR-IN-CHIEF OF COLLECTIVE HUB

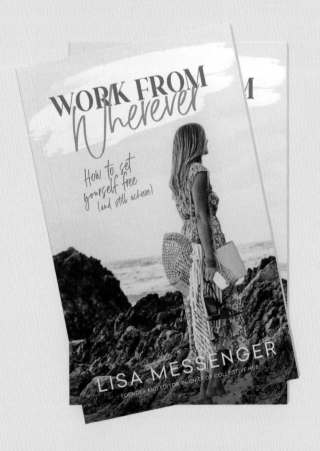

Collect all of Lisa Messenger's books!
Buy your copy at **www.collectivehub.com**

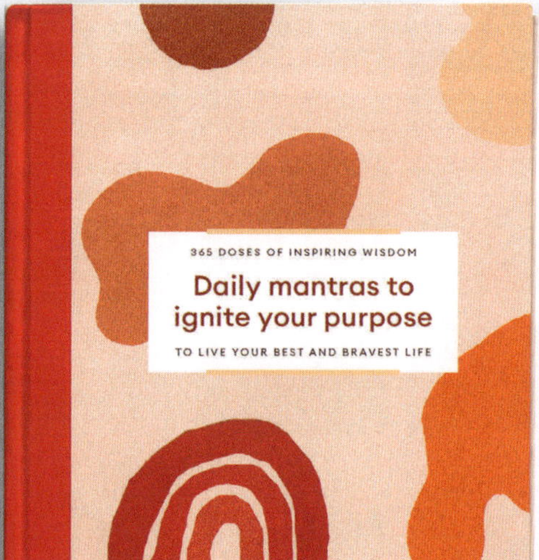
365 DOSES OF INSPIRING WISDOM
Daily mantras to ignite your purpose
TO LIVE YOUR BEST AND BRAVEST LIFE
LISA MESSENGER
FOUNDER AND EDITOR-IN-CHIEF OF COLLECTIVE HUB

Learn from yesterday. Cherish today.
Dream big for tomorrow.

Thoughtfully curated by entrepreneur, author and speaker Lisa Messenger, these artfully presented quotes can be used as meditations, as musings, or as your daily dose of inspiration; one for each day of the year. Every daily message includes a quote, followed by Lisa's personal take, and an affirmation that will help you to step into and ground your courage, spirit, wisdom and, with that, make every day count.

Buy your copy today
www.collectivehub.com

DAILY GRATITUDES

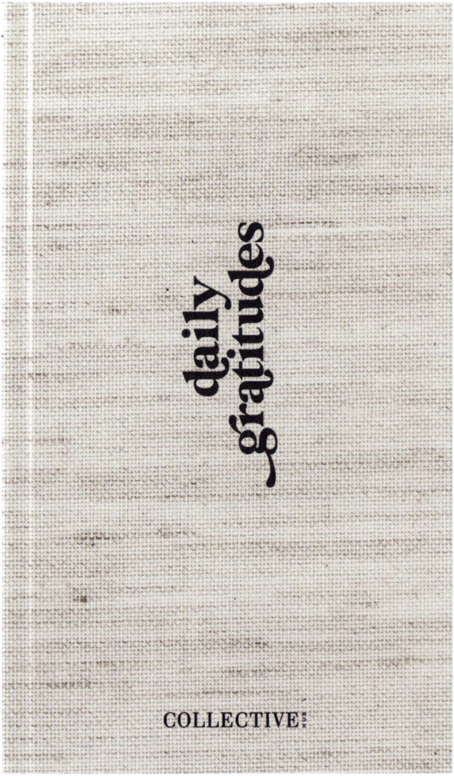
daily gratitudes
COLLECTIVE

Collective Hub's *Daily Gratitudes Planner* includes everything you need to create solid routines and be more grateful in every aspect of your life.

Available from
www.collectivehub.com

COLLECTIVE HUB MAGAZINE

Collective Hub launched in 2013 as a print magazine in 37 countries, and quickly became a global sensation.

The brand evolved into a true international multimedia business and lifestyle platform that encompassed engaging digital content, bespoke events, strategic collaborations and unique product extensions.

Across it all, *Collective Hub*'s vision and purpose was to ignite human potential, and this mission will continue in any form the brand takes. Everything we produce exists to inspire and educate people on how to become the best versions of themselves, so that no human potential goes wasted.

Combining style and substance with a fresh perspective on the issues that matter most, *Collective Hub* covered business, design, technology, social change, fashion, travel, food, film and art.

More than anything, *Collective Hub* was created to bring game-changers, thought-leaders, style-makers, entrepreneurs and intrapreneurs together. We offer pragmatism and inspiration in equal measure to help create a world of dreamers and doers. Join our community and unlock the best version of yourself.

To secure any back issues of *Collective Hub* magazine head to collectivehub.com
@collectivehub #collectivehub

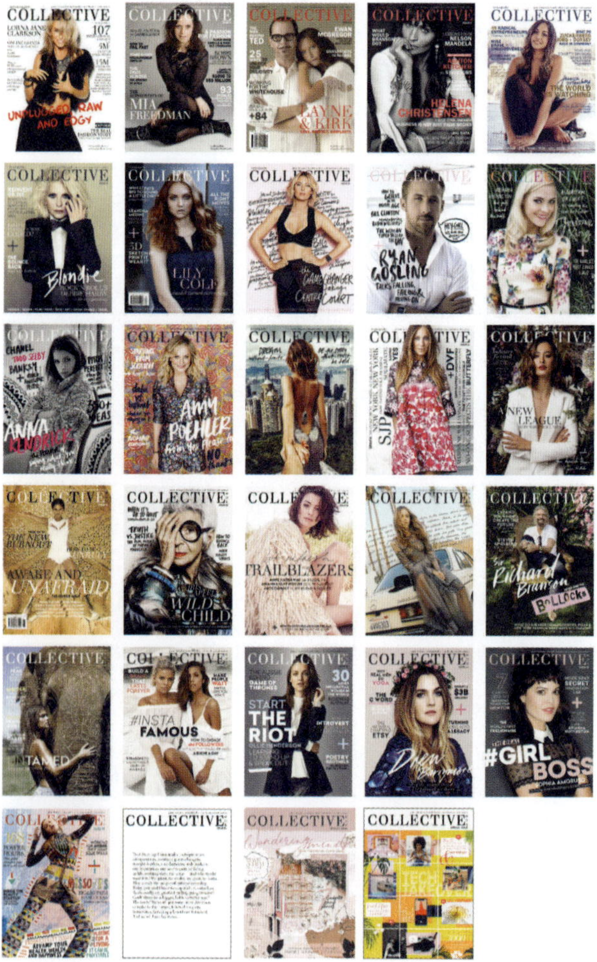
COLLECTIVE
UNPLUGGED, RAW AND EDGY
MIA FREEDMAN
LAYNE & KIRK
HELENA CHRISTENSEN
NELSON MANDELA
THE WORLD IS WATCHING
Blondie
LILY COLE
RYAN GOSLING
ANNA KENDRICK
AMY POEHLER
SJP
+DVF
A NEW LEAGUE
AWAKE AND UNAFRAID
WILD CHILD
TRAILBLAZERS
Sir Richard Branson
BOLLOCKS
UNTAMED
#INSTA FAMOUS
START THE RIOT
#GIRL BOSS
SOPHIA AMORUSO

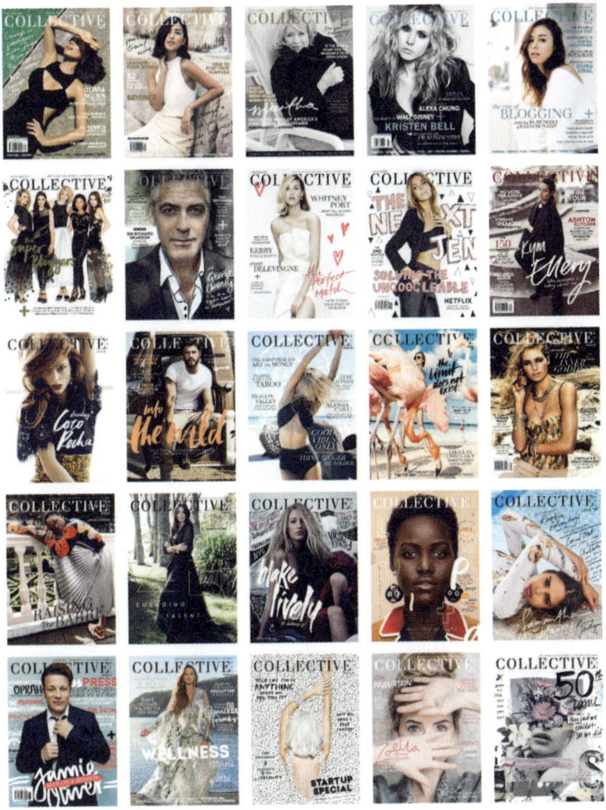
COLLECTIVE
ALEXA CHUNG
WALT DISNEY
KRISTEN BELL
BLOGGING
WHITNEY PORT
KERRY
DELEVINGNE
NETFLIX
TABOO
EMERGING TALENT
OPRAH
PRESS
WELLNESS
STARTUP SPECIAL

CREATE YOUR BEST LIFE JOURNAL

Collective Hub's *Create Your Best Life Journal*, includes everything you need to achieve your ultimate dream life.

Available from
www.collectivehub.com

THE ULTIMATE GUIDE TO SOCIAL MEDIA MARKETING

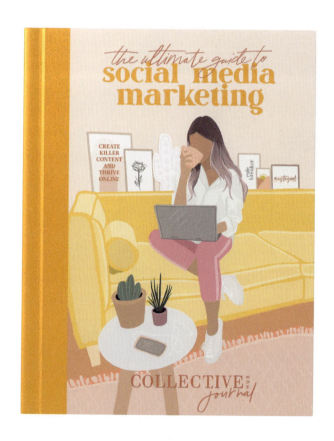

Collective Hub's Ultimate Guide To Social Media Marketing Journal, includes everything you need to create killer content and thrive online.

Available from
www.collectivehub.com

THE NOW OF WORK DIGITAL MASTERCLASS

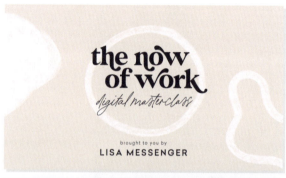

Loved this book?
Dive a little deeper by registering
for Lisa Messenger's The Now of Work
digital masterclass!

Available from
www.collectivehub.com

COLLECTIVE HUB JOURNALS

Love to write or travel?
Check out our *Collective Hub* journals/planners!
Including *The Ultimate Writer's Journal*,
and *The Ultimate Travel Journal*.

Available from
www.collectivehub.com

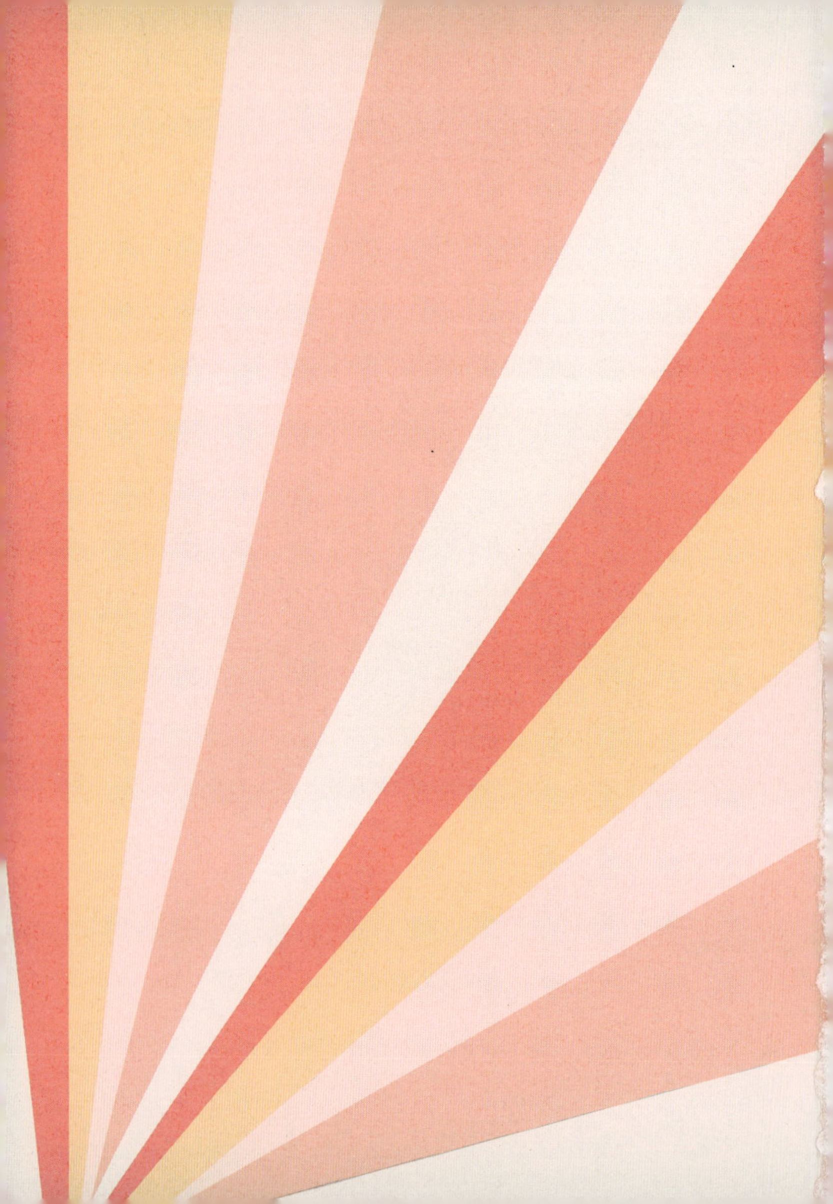

> We can't be afraid of change. You may feel very secure in the pond that you are in, but if you never venture out of it, you will never know that there is such a thing as an ocean, a sea. Holding onto something that is good for you now, may be the very reason why you don't have something better.

— C. JOYBELL C

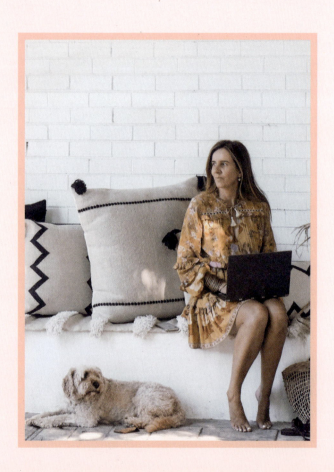